THE **AT◊WAR** SERIES

TIGER TANKS
AT WAR

**MICHAEL GREEN AND
JAMES D. BROWN**

ZENITH PRESS

First published in 2008 by Zenith Press, an imprint of
MBI Publishing Company, 400 First Avenue North,
Suite 300, Minneapolis, MN 55401 USA

Zenith Press titles are also available at discounts in bulk
quantity for industrial or sales-promotional use. For
details write to Special Sales Manager at MBI
Publishing Company, 400 First Avenue North, Suite
300, Minneapolis, MN 55401 USA.

To find out more about our books, join us online at
www.zenithpress.com.

Library of Congress Cataloging-in-Publication Data

Green, Michael.
 Tiger tanks at war / by Michael Green and James D.
Brown.
   p. cm.
 ISBN-13: 978-0-7603-3112-5 (softbound)
 ISBN-10: 0-7603-3112-X (softbound)
 1. Tiger (Tank) I. Brown, James D. II. Title.
UG446.5.G6945 2008
623.7'4762—dc22
                 2007015664

About the authors:
Michael Green is a freelance writer, researcher, and
photographer who specializes in military,
transportation, and law enforcement subjects. His many
books include *M2/M3 Bradley at War*, *M4 Sherman at
War*, and *Panzers at War*, all published by Zenith Press.
Green has also written numerous articles for a variety of
national and international military-related magazines.

James D. Brown served twenty years in the U.S. Army as
an armor officer with a secondary specialty in research
and development. His active duty service includes a
four-year tour as an assistant professor of engineering
at the United States Military Academy, where he taught
combat vehicle design and automotive engineering.

On the cover:
(main) The only running Tiger E tank in the world
today. *David Marian*

(inset) The Tiger B tank had well-sloped armor, in
contrast to the Tiger E. *David Marian*

On the frontispiece: An abandoned Tiger E tank.
Patton Museum

On the title pages: A Tiger B tank. *Andreas Kirchoff*

On the back cover: A late-model production Tiger E
tank. *Bob Fleming*

Editor: Steve Gansen
Designer: Brenda C. Canales

Printed in Singapore

CONTENTS

ACKNOWLEDGMENTS

In addition to those mentioned in the text and photo credits of this book, special thanks are due to the very helpful staffs of the U.S. Army's Patton Museum of Cavalry and Armor, Fort Knox, Kentucky; the Tank Museum, Bovington, England; and the U.S. Army Ordnance Museum, Aberdeen, Maryland. Individuals who made an extra effort in assisting the authors but do not appear in the text or photo caption credits include Jacques Littlefield, Randy Talbot, Richard Hunnicutt, Dean and Nancy Kleffman, David Fletcher, Ron Hare, and Richard Cox.

INTRODUCTION

The Tiger tanks produced by Germany during World War II are legendary. As with all legends, however, there is as much myth as truth in their story. Part of their mystique originated during the war, when what little information the Germans gave out was tinged for propaganda purposes. The inflated German accounts were somewhat offset by Allied versions, which tended to understate their capabilities. As we shall see in the chapters that follow, both sides had good reason to withhold the truth, for while the Tigers were not as good as the Germans had hoped they would be, they were far more formidable than the Allies had feared.

With the Panzer V ("Panther"), the Tigers were the first German tanks designed uncompromisingly as antitank platforms. Earlier German tanks were originally the product of tradeoffs, particularly in their armament, of a school of thought that considered dedicated antitank guns as the principal counter to enemy tanks. Only after some bitterly earned combat lessons did the Germans come to consider armor-defeating capability as the prime attribute of a tank gun. Ironically, the Tigers were armed with variants of an antiaircraft gun that was pressed into service as an antitank weapon when the Germans encountered unexpectedly heavily armored French tanks in what was otherwise an easy victory in the battle of France.

The Tigers are actually two distinct tanks, related by little more than the bore diameter of their guns, the basic design of their engines, and the curiously shared common title Panzer VI. The later Tiger B can in no way be considered a product-improved Tiger E, and it remains something of a mystery why they shared a common name. The Tiger E was a scaled-up expression of the armored-box-on-a-suspension architecture that had produced Panzers I through IV, and indeed, most contemporary Allied tanks. Although structurally easy to design and produce, the boxy hull took no advantage of the well-known properties of sloped armor and relied instead on raw-boned mass, and plenty of it, for its protection. Tiger B was a more modern concept, benefiting indirectly from the Russian T-34 design and much more directly from the Panther. Tiger E had an 88mm gun whose chamber design was almost identical to its antiaircraft antecedent. Tiger B's gun was not only considerably longer but fired a larger cartridge that was not interchangeable with those from a Tiger E. Although their suspensions may appear related, the eight-axle interleaved suspension of Tiger E was redesigned as a nine-axle overlapped layout on Tiger B.

Neither tank was a strategic success; both were far more heavily armed than their adversaries were. This allowed them to score kills at greater ranges. Both featured heavier armor, which allowed them to absorb hits. Tactically, they were nearly invincible, however, neither could be produced in sufficient quantity to strategically swing the war to the German side, and neither was mechanically reliable enough to sustain their tactical advantages. The development and fielding of both was heavily influenced by the personal interference of a crazed dictator, and it may be argued that the Germans would have been better off to concentrate on the production and further development of the Panther.

What is inarguable, though, is that the Tigers brought a new dimension to warfare and that their presence in the German arsenal engendered an Allied response in both tactics and material development of tanks, which far outlasted the Nazis and is reflected even today in armies around the world. The legend of the Tigers was indeed as much myth as fact, but the central fact is that they were some of the most important designs in the history of armored warfare.

With that said, the authors would also like to point out that this book is not the definitive technical or combat history of the Tiger tanks. Rather, the authors have strived to provide the reader a better understanding of how the vehicles and their crews actually functioned in combat, within the publisher's size and format restrictions.

This Somua 35 French army medium tank belongs to the collection of the U.S. Army Ordnance Museum. Armed with a turret-mounted 47mm main gun and two 7.5mm machine guns, it featured both a cast-steel armored hull and turret and was far superior to the German medium tanks in many ways. *Michael Green*

Belonging to the Military Vehicle Technology Foundation is a two-man Panzer I light tank, powered by a Krupp gasoline engine. Subsequent versions of the vehicle featured Maybach gasoline engines. The Panzer I light tank was the most numerous vehicle in the German army inventory through the 1930s. *Michael Green*

CHAPTER ONE

BACKGROUND AND DESCRIPTION

AS WITH SO MANY OTHER WARTIME TANK DESIGNS, the development and fielding of the German Tiger tanks did not result from studied thought on the future needs of the German army. Rather, they appeared on the field of battle in response to tanks or antitank guns used by their enemies. In many respects, the results were not always in the best interest of the German army.

After World War I, the French army developed a number of heavy tank designs featuring armor thick enough to make them invulnerable to all existing German antitank guns. However, the massive armor severely compromised maneuverability, a critical capability in warfare. With memories of elaborate trench warfare campaigns fresh in their minds, the French envisioned a new paradigm of warfare in which armored forces would push their way through the most extensive trench systems and be invulnerable to the inevitable hits. What the French failed to appreciate was that speed and maneuverability could also defeat trench-bound armies by advancing to the front faster than the soldiers dug trenches. As we shall see, the French army's emphasis on armor protection and firepower at the expense of mobility found itself repeated by the German army and became a major deficiency of the Tiger tanks.

In anticipation of a future clash with their traditional French foe, the German army's chief of the Ordnance Department issued a report in October 1935 that set down the requirements for a new tank. It would feature a turret-mounted 75mm main gun firing a projectile that could penetrate the French army's heavy tank armor.

A turret-mounted 75mm gun on a tank with armor almost an inch thick would require German industry to design a new tank weighing more than thirty tons. At that time, the only German army tank in widespread service was the six-ton PzKpfw I. The designation PzKpfw stood for *PanzerKampfwagen* ("armored fighting vehicle") hereafter referred to as "Panzer" in the text.

A PROBLEM APPEARS

The first version of the Panzer I light tank had armor less than one-half-inch thick. Armament consisted only of two turret-mounted 7.92mm machine guns. In 1935, German industry had trouble building sufficient numbers of even these light tanks, and the new heavy tank appeared to be an impossible burden. The Panzer I had entered service with the German army in 1934 and rendered important service as a training vehicle during the rebuilding of the armored force. Future Panzer leaders, from platoon

On display at the French army tank museum is this four-man Char B1 *bis* heavy tank armed with a turret-mounted high-velocity 47mm gun and a low-velocity front hull–mounted 75mm gun traversed by turning the entire vehicle. In addition to the two cannons, the vehicle featured three 7.5mm machine guns. *Christophe Vallier*

leaders to corps commanders, had learned the basics of maneuver warfare in the humble Panzer I.

The initial model of the roughly eight-ton Panzer II light tank entered into German army service in 1937. The three-man Panzer II light tank featured a turret-mounted 20mm automatic cannon as its main gun and had heavier armor than its predecessor, the Panzer I. However, although useful as a light tank, it was not capable of taking on the French tanks of the day.

The Panzer III also appeared in German army service in 1937. The five-man medium tank mounted a 37mm tank-killing main gun, upgraded in later models to a 50mm main gun.

A third tank, the first German 75mm main gun–equipped tank, the Panzer IV, also appeared in 1937. The five-man medium tank came with a 75mm howitzer intended to deal with only towed antitank guns and defensive positions. The Panzer IV supported the Panzer I and II light tanks as well as the Panzer III medium tank. In later models, the Panzer IV appeared with a long-barreled 75mm gun, which made it a tank killer.

Howitzers tend to be short-barreled, low-velocity cannons, generally employed as indirect-fire artillery weapons, firing high-explosive (HE) projectiles in a curved trajectory (flight path). Although the term *gun* generally applies to all firearms, within the military, its use is more restricted and in technical sense refers to a cannon with a relatively long barrel, a higher muzzle velocity (the speed of the projectile in flight) than a howitzer's projectiles, a very flat trajectory (flight path), and a more limited maximum elevation than a howitzer.

World War II began on September 1, 1939, with the German army invasion of Poland. The Polish army possessed a number of light tanks of foreign and indigenous design along with small-caliber towed antitank guns. This combination inflicted moderate losses on the German army's Panzer I and II series light tanks and the sixteen-ton Panzer III and twenty-one-ton IV series medium tanks.

This battlefield experience resulted in an up-armoring of the Panzer III and IV series medium tanks

The British Matilda II infantry support tank armed with a 40mm main gun featured armor protection up to three inches thick. The thickness of the tank's armor made it immune to almost all the German army tank and antitank guns in the battle for France in the summer of 1940. *Michael Green*

The T34/76 medium tank was a shock to the German army during its invasion of the Soviet Union. The tank's armor made it proof against German tank and antitank guns, except at extremely close range. The 76.2mm main gun on the T34/76 easily penetrated the armor on German tanks. *Michael Green*

from one-half inch to a full inch of armor. The German army was then confident that their medium tanks were more than adequately armed and armored for any future military operations. That view would change with the successful German army invasion of France in the summer of 1940.

Although the German army did eventually prevail over their unprepared opponents in the short battle of France, the Germans discovered that a number of French and British tanks mounted enough armor protection to resist German tank and antitank (AT) fire. The standard German 37mm guns fired an armor-piercing (AP) projectile weighing less than one pound with a muzzle velocity of 2,495 feet per second. In theory, the weapon could penetrate about an inch and a half of armor sloped at 30 degrees at a range of four hundred yards.

The enemy tanks that caused the German army problems during the invasion of France included the four-man, thirty-ton, British Matilda II infantry support tank; the three-man, twenty-two-ton, French Somua 35 medium tank; and the four-man, thirty-five-ton, French Char B1 *bis* heavy tank. These same British and French tanks also mounted weapons that had no problem penetrating the armor on the German army's light and medium tanks. French and British towed antitank guns also took a toll on the German tanks.

The British Matilda II had a turret-mounted 40mm main gun that fired a two-pound AP projectile at a muzzle velocity of 2,600 feet per second. In theory, it could penetrate about two inches of armor at a range of five hundred yards. The maximum armor thickness on the British Matilda tank was just a bit more than three inches.

Both the French Somua medium tank and the Char B1 *bis* heavy tank had a maximum armor thickness of a little more than two inches. The 47mm main gun in the Somua and Char B1 *bis* turrets fired a three-pound AP projectile at a muzzle velocity of 2,300 feet per second. The 75mm hull-mounted gun on the front of the Char B1 *bis* fired a fourteen-pound AP projectile with a high-explosive element. Both the 47mm and 75mm guns could, in theory, penetrate more than an inch and a half of armor, sloped at 30 degrees, at a range of just more than four hundred yards.

The belated discovery of the firepower and armor protection inferiority of the German tanks during the battle for France led the German army to question earlier assumptions concerning their opponents' tanks and towed AT guns. Work quickly began on further upgrading the firepower and armor protection levels of their Panzer III and IV medium tanks.

A SOLUTION APPEARS

Hitler believed the obvious—that a new heavily armed and armored heavy tank was the solution. The German army Ordnance Department had dismissed the idea of a heavy tank because of the tactical problems inherent with road, rail, and bridge weight restrictions within Europe. To placate Hitler, the weapon design office of the German army Ordnance Department commissioned noted automotive engineer Dr. Ferdinand Porsche to design a heavy tank chassis in the autumn of 1940.

In a May 1941 meeting, Hitler, having lost his patience with the German army Ordnance Department's lack of progress in fielding a heavy tank, took personal charge of the project. He awarded Porsche and the German firm of Henschel & Sohn, a builder of train locomotives, contracts for the building of a small number of prototype heavy tank chassis to be ready for his inspection on April 20, 1942. The contract for the

The Red Army KV-1 heavy tank mounted the same 76.2mm main gun as found on the T34/76 medium tank and boasted much thicker armor that made it even harder to kill by German tank and antitank guns. Only the German 88mm antiaircraft gun had a chance of penetrating the KV-1's thick armor hide. *Michael Green*

design and building of the turret for the new heavy tank went to Krupp, the famous arms builder. The new heavy tank requirements called for frontal armor of five inches thick and side armor of two inches thick. The main gun was required to penetrate at least four inches of armor at 1,371 yards.

An added impetus to the German army's development and fielding of a heavy tank was the German invasion of the Soviet Union in June 1941. Encounters with Soviet army (known as the Red Army at the time) tank units uncovered the fact that the armor on their four-man T34/76 medium tank and their five-man KV heavy tank series was able to defeat all of the German tank and antitank guns on the battlefield.

In addition, the twenty-six-ton T34/76 and the fifty-two-ton KV-1 mounted a 76.2mm main gun whose AP projectile easily penetrated German tank armor. The fourteen-pound AP projectile, with a muzzle velocity of 2,200 feet per second could punch through more than two inches of armor at one thousand yards. Another projectile with a seven-pound sub-caliber tungsten-carbide core fired at 3,200 feet per second could penetrate even heavier armor.

The German army managed to overcome their technical inferiority with superior tactics because they encountered only small numbers of the T34/76 medium and KV-1 heavy tanks during the first few months of their campaign in Russia. They also accelerated the development and fielding of up-armored and up-gunned versions of the Panzer III and IV medium tanks as a countermeasure to the unexpected Red Army tanks. Frontal armor thickness of the Panzer III increased to more than two inches and the Panzer IV frontal armor thickness went up to three inches.

The Porsche-designed chassis for the German army's heavy tank competition appears on a forest trail during mobility testing. Dr. Ferdinand Porsche loved to innovate and came up with some very interesting concepts for his vehicle, including a gasoline-electric drivetrain. However, the rush to field a heavy tank left little time to work the bugs out of his untested concepts. *Patton Museum*

The Tank Museum, located at Bovington, England, has the only running Tiger E tank in the world today. Captured by the British army in North Africa, in April 1943, the vehicle then went off to England for extensive testing. It became part of the museum's collection after World War II and remains its most popular exhibit. *David Marian*

A DECISION IS NEEDED

By late 1940, both Porsche and Henschel had acquired the engineering talent to produce a heavy tank design that would meet Hitler's requirements. Dr. Ferdinand Porsche was so convinced that he would win the competition over Henschel, owing to his superior product and his close friendship with Hitler, that he started production without a contract. Porsche contracted with Krupp to build one hundred chassis to his design specifications and one hundred Krupp-designed turrets for the chassis. The new tank was designated VK 45.01 (P) denoting Porsche Version 01 of a full-tracked motor vehicle (Vollkettenkraftfahrzeug) weighing forty-five metric tonnes (49.6 tons).

While Hitler had favored the mounting of a Rheinmetall-Borsig 88mm gun, the Krupp turret was incapable of mounting the large, heavy gun. The compromise was the somewhat less-capable Krupp 88mm gun, based on the 8.8cm FlaK antiaircraft guns already in service with the German military.

Meanwhile, Henschel had been working on a heavy tank weighing less than forty tons for the German army. The emerging roughly fifty-ton requirement caught them by surprise and forced them to cobble available components together in order to meet Hitler's deadline. Henschel's new prototype heavy tank chassis was designated the VK 45.01 (H).

The Porsche and Henschel chassis fell under a procurement project referred to as the *Tiger-Programm*. The vehicle went through a number of designation changes during the rapid gestation period of the new heavy tank. The first "Tiger tank" reference occurred in

The engine exhaust system on the Tiger E tank consisted of two jacketed exhaust pipes mounted on the rear hull plate of the vehicle. The lower portion of these jacketed pipes featured cast armored fixtures protecting them from enemy fire at the point they projected through the tank's rear hull armor plate. A noise muffler attached to the top of the jacketed exhaust pipes. To hide the glowing hot exhaust pipes from enemy observation, sheet metal guards often covered them. *Andreas Kirchoff*

February 1942 when it appeared in German military documents as the Tiger H1. The following month it appeared as the Panzer VI (VK 45.01/H) Ausf. H1 (Tiger). The abbreviation *Ausf.* stands for the German word *Ausfuhrung* and refers to a specific model of a vehicle.

On April 20, 1942, Porsche and Henschel presented their respective Tiger tank chassis to Hitler, both fitted with Krupp turrets. Although neither vehicle was quite ready for production, it was clear that the Henschel prototype chassis was superior. Among its defects, the Porsche chassis suffered a number of engine compartment fires during the demonstration. After the demonstrations, Hitler turned to Albert Speer, his *Reichsminister* (civilian minister of armament), to arrange for testing of the two prototype Tiger tank chassis to see which best met the requirements.

This summary of the decision process for picking a winning contender between the Porsche and Henschel candidate Tiger tank chassis appears in *Tiger: The History of a Legendary Weapon 1942–1945*, a book written by Egon Kleine and Volkmar Kuhn.

[Albert] Speer gave Oberst [Colonel] Thomale, who until the end of March had been the commanding officer of the 27th Panzer Regiment and who had received the Knight's Cross on 10 February 1942, the difficult task of determining which of the two prototypes was best suited for the Panzer units. Oberst Thomale, who since April 1942 had been liaison officer between the Chief of the Replacement Army, Generaloberst Fromm, and Reichsminister Speer, had the Henschel Tiger and several Porsche Tigers brought together at the Berka troop training grounds in May 1942 in order to compare the two types during rigorous trials.

In Berka a panel was organized to evaluate the two types of Tiger tank. Two chairmen were selected: For the military assessment, Oberst Thomale; and for the technical assessment, Professor Ing. von Eberan of the Dresden Institute of Technology. Professor

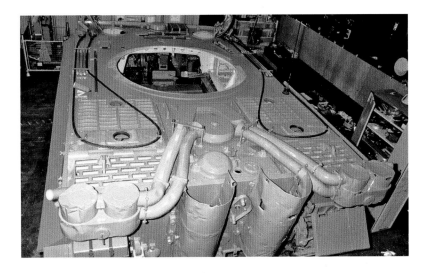

This picture shows the Tank Museum's early model Tiger E tank hull in the restoration shop without its turret. This vehicle is fitted with the add-on Feifel Air Filter system mounted on the right and left upper rear corners of the hull. It also sports sheet metal guards around its rear hull plate–mounted jacketed engine exhaust pipes. *Tank Museum, Bovington*

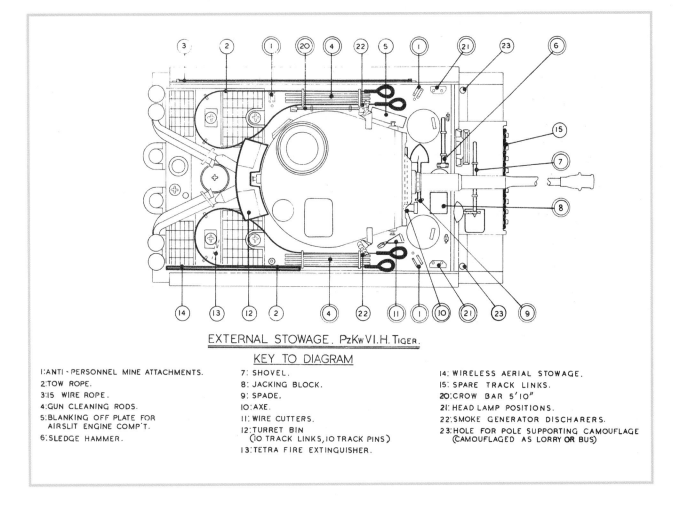

EXTERNAL STOWAGE. PzKw VI.H. TIGER.

KEY TO DIAGRAM

1: ANTI-PERSONNEL MINE ATTACHMENTS.
2: TOW ROPE.
3: 15 WIRE ROPE.
4: GUN CLEANING RODS.
5: BLANKING OFF PLATE FOR AIRSLIT ENGINE COMP'T.
6: SLEDGE HAMMER.

7: SHOVEL.
8: JACKING BLOCK.
9: SPADE.
10: AXE.
11: WIRE CUTTERS.
12: TURRET BIN (10 TRACK LINKS, 10 TRACK PINS)
13: TETRA FIRE EXTINGUISHER.

14: WIRELESS AERIAL STOWAGE.
15: SPARE TRACK LINKS.
20: CROW BAR 5'10"
21: HEAD LAMP POSITIONS.
22: SMOKE GENERATOR DISCHARERS.
23: HOLE FOR POLE SUPPORTING CAMOUFLAGE (CAMOUFLAGED AS LORRY OR BUS)

From a British army report on the Tiger E tank is this overhead line drawing showing the location of many of the external components of the vehicle. As with most tanks, some of the external components were changed or moved around on later production vehicles in response to production needs or user feedback.

A close-up view of an early model Tiger E tank shows the original drum-type armored tank commander's cupola. It came with five vision slits arrayed around its circumference. Behind the slits were replaceable ballistic glass blocks, about four inches thick, used to protect the vehicle commander from battlefield projectiles and fragments. The hatch cover of this cupola projected upward when opened and drew unwanted attention from snipers and antitank guns. *Andreas Kirchoff*

Ing. von Eberan had brought along a large number of his technical advisors.

The most important military demand of the new Panzer was that the vehicle should be available in large numbers by the beginning of summer 1943 at the latest. Following extensive testing the Henschel Tiger was unanimously chosen as the superior of the two tanks. The electric drive of the Porsche Tiger was highly interesting, but it was much too complicated to be serviced with the simple means available to the front-line units, especially in the Russian theatre.

In Reichsminister Speer's presence, Oberst Thomale reported the panel's findings to Hitler and explained the reasons behind its decision. Hitler was obviously irritated that it was not Professor Porsche, the genial inventor and designer of the Volkswagen, but the Henschel firm that was suggested for production. On the following day, however, Hitler once again ordered both men to him and agreed on the proposed solution.

Most of the one hundred chassis that Krupp built for Porsche later appeared as tank destroyers, with a casemated 88mm main gun. Three saw use as armored recovery vehicles, and the rest were set aside for experimental purposes. Most of the Krupp-designed and -built turrets ordered by Porsche for their canceled heavy tank contender went through a modifying process to fit them to the Henschel production chassis.

PRODUCTION BEGINS

The first Tiger tank rolled off the Henschel production line in August 1942. The production designation became Panzer VI H (8.8cm) (SdKfz 182) Ausf. H. The abbreviation SdKfz stands for Sonderkraftfahrzeug, which translates to "special motor vehicle" and refers to the vehicle's ordnance inventory number. The designation changed to Panzer (Tiger 8.8cm L/56) SdKfz 181 Ausf. E in early March 1943, or Tiger E for short. At the same time, the unofficial name "Tiger I" tank came into use, which is the name most often used even today. The

Beginning in July 1943, a new low-profile tank commander's cupola, as seen here, began appearing on Tiger E tanks with an attachment rail for a 7.92mm machine gun. This new cast armor cupola featured seven periscopes arrayed around its circumference that had external armored hoods. The hatch cover pivoted to open, and thus did not project above the tank. *Frank Schulz*

Western Allies tended to refer to the vehicle as the Mark VI in their written reports.

In addition to the standard production version of the Tiger E tank, Henschel produced two different command versions (*Panzerbefehlswagen*) with different radio arrangements and antennas—one a radio setup in order to communicate with ground support aircraft and the other, higher headquarters out of the range of the standard tank-mounted radio sets. The additional radios reduced the available space for main gun rounds and small-arms ammunition. The machine gun fitted to fire alongside the main gun disappeared in the command versions, designated the SdKfz 267 and SdKfz 268.

TIGER E TANK DESCRIPTION

On January 16, 1943, the Red Army captured an intact Tiger E tank and subjected it to extensive testing to uncover any weak points they could exploit in battle. The British army captured its first intact Tiger E tank on April 21, 1943, in North Africa. They discovered that the Tiger's combat weight was fifty-six tons, a jump in weight compared to the original roughly fifty-ton design limit. Weight gain is common to almost all tank designs and reflected the emphasis by Hitler and the German army on providing the tank with a suitable level of armor protection for its role on the battlefield.

The British army measured their first captured Tiger E tank's hull as twenty feet eight and one-half inches long. The front overhang of the main gun increased the length to twenty-seven feet nine inches. The overall width of the vehicle, including the mudguards, was twelve feet three inches. The vehicle was nine feet four and one-half inches high.

After a close study of the captured Tiger E tank, a number of detailed reports on the tank's design and construction were passed on to the U.S. Army. A passage from one of those original reports describes the most noticeable external features of the vehicle.

As compared with other AFVs in service [summer 1943], the Tiger is outstandingly well armed and protected. Designed to carry an 8.8cm gun and constructed of very heavy armor plate, the vehicle is naturally of exceptional size and weight and it is therefore somewhat surprising to note how it is, to a certain degree, dwarfed by the main armament. Viewed from the side with the turret at 12 o'clock, the 8.8 cm gun extends beyond the nose of the tank by about a quarter of its length, and the length from the muzzle brake to the mantlet [gun shield] is rather over half the total length of the vehicle.

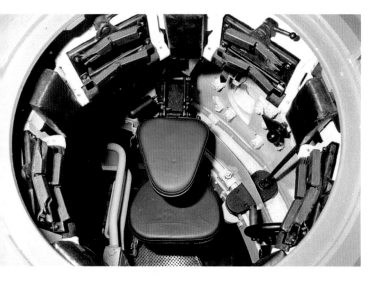

Looking down the tank commander's hatch on a Tiger E tank, featuring the original drum-type cupola, both of the commander's seats are visible. The upper seat allowed the tank commander to sit and to look out over the top of his cupola, while the lower seat allowed him to sit and look out through the vision slits of the cupola. *Tank Museum, Bovington*

Barrel length plays an important part in the transfer of energy from the propellant charge to an AP projectile. The more speed a projectile has when leaving a gun barrel, referred to as muzzle velocity, the faster and harder it will strike an opponent's armor.

A feature that surprised British army personnel that examined the early production Tiger E tank captured in North Africa was a system that allowed it to run submerged in water up to fifteen feet deep. The deep water–fording capability was critical to the development of the Tiger E tank, as it eliminated the need for the vehicles to cross the many bridges with thirty-ton weight limits. As events progressed, the Germans discovered that the deep water–fording equipment was of limited practical value, and it disappeared from production vehicles beginning in August 1943.

TANK COMMANDER

In battle, a Tiger E tank commander controlled the movement and fire of his vehicle. His effectiveness in battle was dependent on how well he and his crew worked together, and when a target appeared, the tank commander decided whether to engage the target. The

Visible looking down through the tank commander's hatch on a Tiger E tank is the commander's lower seat position. The upper seat folds down and acts as a backrest while the commander sits on the lower seat. To the upper right-hand side of the picture is his manually operated hand-wheel for turning the turret. *Tank Museum, Bovington*

tank commander also decided which weapon to use and the type of ammunition that would most effectively destroy the target. This decision depended on the type of target (tank, infantry, antitank gun, or pillbox), the range to the target, and a thorough knowledge of the capabilities and limitations of the vehicle's onboard weapons and the type and quantity of ammunition available.

A Tiger E tank manual advises the tank commander: "Your quick thinking, your certain commands, brings the tank to life. Your rapid directions in selecting the warhead (armor piercing, high explosive, etc.) has a decisive effect. You hold all the trump cards in your hands. Now learn to play the game!"

Otto Carius, a highly decorated Tiger E tank ace who saw heavy combat on the Eastern Front, describes his feelings on one aspect of what made a successful Tiger tank commander in his 1960 book titled *Tiger im Schlamm* (*Tiger in the Mud*):

> The personal aggressiveness of the commander while observing was decisive for success against numerically vastly superior enemy formations. The lack of good observation by the Russians often resulted in the defeat of large units. Tank commanders who slam their hatches shut at the beginning of an attack and don't open them again until the objective has been reached are useless, or at least second rate.

A British army report on the Tiger E tank goes into detail on the tank commander's position within the vehicle:

> For the first time, the [tank] commander's position is offset to the nearside [left] behind the gunner. A pressed sheet metal guard plate is bolted to the roof of the turret on the commander's right hand side, which protects him from the left deflector [recoil] guard side plate and possible injury to his right elbow by the recoil of the gun.
>
> The commander's seat is mounted on a pillar bolted to the turret ring at 7 o'clock. There are two seats on the same pillar, one above the other. The upper one [fifty-two inches above the turret platform] is used for observing out of the top of the cupola and when not in use may be folded down to

Looking down through the tank commander's hatch on a Tiger E tank, the commander's lower seat position is visible at the bottom of the picture. Just below and slightly in front of the commander's seat is the gunner's seat position. To the right of the tank commander is the sheet metal guard that protects him from any main gun back-blast when the breech opens. *Tank Museum, Bovington*

form the backrest of the lower seat, by operating a lever on the right hand side of the pillar against the compression of a spring. The lower seat [thirty-six inches above the turret platform] may be folded up when not in use.

Combat experience showed that the pressed sheet metal guard hindered the verbal communication between the Tiger E tank commander and loader. To correct this, a fireproof cloth blanket replaced the metal guard plate in new production tanks after July 1943. Earlier production Tiger E tanks had the fireproof cloth blankets retrofitted to them when available.

Berent Isenberg, a Tiger E tank gunner in Italy, remembers that his tank never had any obstruction between the loader on one side of the vehicle's turret and the tank commander and him on the other side of the turret.

The lower of two footrests for the Tiger E tank commander was located on the gunner's seat below and behind the seat cushion. The higher footrest attached to the post behind the gunner's seat backrest. The Tiger E tank commander used the lower footrest when his seat was in the lower position and the upper footrest when the seat was in the upper position.

A small, manually operated hand-wheel to the left of the Tiger E tank commander position allowed him to turn the turret. Before the commander could turn the turret with the hand-wheel, the gunner had to release a latch on his hand-wheel. This prevented the commander from inadvertently interfering with the gunner's aim.

Another British army report describes the vision arrangement of the tank commander's early production eighteen-inch-diameter cupola on the Tiger E tank:

The [tank] commander is provided with five horizontal slits giving all round vision. The slits are equally spaced around the cupola and measure 7 1/4 inch by 5/8 inch. No shutters are provided for those [three-and-one-half-inch thick replaceable laminated glass block] visors, [and] a sighting strip is fitted to the foremost visor.

A more detailed British military report on the observation devices in the original Tiger E tank cupola sums up the opinions of those on the vehicle:

In the early models of the Tiger, it appears that the designers did not consider near vision to be so important. The commander's cupola is placed not centrally behind [as on the PzKpfw III and IV medium tanks], but to one side of the gun. Vision to the left and rear of the turret is good, but bad to the

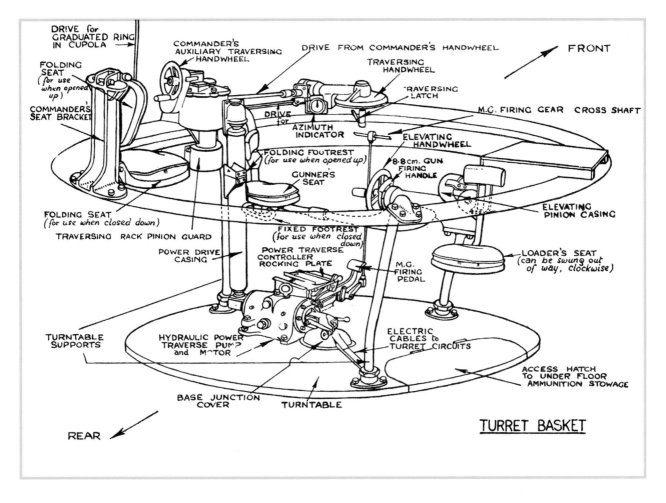

DRIVE for GRADUATED RING IN CUPOLA

FOLDING SEAT (for use when opened up)

COMMANDER'S SEAT BRACKET

COMMANDER'S AUXILIARY TRAVERSING HANDWHEEL

DRIVE FROM COMMANDER'S HANDWHEEL

TRAVERSING HANDWHEEL

FRONT

TRAVERSING LATCH

M.C. FIRING GEAR   CROSS SHAFT

DRIVE for AZIMUTH INDICATOR

ELEVATING HANDWHEEL

FOLDING FOOTREST (for use when opened up)

GUNNER'S SEAT

8·8cm. GUN FIRING HANDLE

ELEVATING PINION CASING

FOLDING SEAT (for use when closed down)

TRAVERSING RACK PINION GUARD

POWER DRIVE CASING

FIXED FOOTREST (for use when closed down)

POWER TRAVERSE CONTROLLER ROCKING PLATE

M.G. FIRING PEDAL

LOADER'S SEAT (can be swung out of way, clockwise)

TURNTABLE SUPPORTS

HYDRAULIC POWER TRAVERSE PUMP and MOTOR

ELECTRIC CABLES to TURRET CIRCUITS

ACCESS HATCH TO UNDER FLOOR AMMUNITION STOWAGE

BASE JUNCTION COVER

TURNTABLE

REAR

TURRET BASKET

From a British army report appears this illustration of the Tiger E tank turret basket, with all its components listed. It attached to the turret ring at three different points and rotated when the turret was turned. Red Army tanks like the T34 medium tank series did not have a turret basket, forcing the loader to walk around the bottom of the vehicle's hull floor as the turret turned. *Tank Museum, Bovington*

right and right rear. It should, however, be noted that part of the blind area to the right in the commander's field can be seen through the loader's [vision] slot.

A Red Army antitank weapon tore off the cupola of Otto Carius' Tiger E tank. He then pointed out a flaw in the original design of the tank commander's cupola:

I wouldn't have been the first one that this had happened to. The reason could be found in a design failure. On the initial "Tiger," the cupola was still welded. It rose up high and had direct vision slits. The cupola hatch stood up vertically when it was opened. Thus, from a distance, anyone could recognize that the tank was vulnerable from the top.

A high explosive round only had to hit the hatch, and the entire charge then came down on the commander's head. If a commander wanted to close the opened hatch, he had to lean over on the outside of the vehicle and expose himself to the hip to unhitch a safety latch that released it. This faulty design was soon changed. Thereafter, the cupola was rounded off. The commander looked indirectly through the vision slits with periscopes, and the hatch swung right horizontally and closed.

Based on user feedback, Krupp came up with a new low-profile, circular, cast armor cupola for the Tiger E tank. It began appearing on production vehicles in July 1943 along with a host of other design improvements.

The Tiger E power traverse did not always offer enough control for good shooting accuracy, so once near the target, the gunner often refined his aim with the hand-wheel visible in the foreground. He could turn it as he looked out through the gun shield with his optical sights (missing in this vehicle although the bracket for mounting them remains). The gun mount is at the right in this view. *Frank Schulz*

In addition, the new commander's cupola featured armor hoods over the seven periscopes and a metal rail around a portion of the top of the cupola for the mounting of an external 7.92mm machine gun. Both types of overhead armored hatch lids featured a handle for opening the hatch from the outside of the vehicle. To prevent enemy combatants from opening the tank commander's cupola hatch lid in combat, there was a hatch lid lock inside the cupola.

GUNNER

The job of a gunner on a World War II tank was to fire and adjust the main gun and coaxial machine gun under the direction of the tank commander. While observation from his position was always limited, he did assist the tank commander in acquiring targets. The gunner entered and exited the vehicle through the vehicle commander's overhead cupola.

A British army report describes the Tiger E tank gunner's position in detail:

The gunner sits in front of the [tank] commander on the left side of the main armament. His seat is elliptically shaped and padded. It is mounted on a horizontal arm and is not adjustable. The backrest is also padded and curved to fit the gunner's back.

The [gunner's manually operated] elevating hand-wheel is mounted on a horizontal shaft passing transversely under the gun. It is nine inches in diameter and situated on the right of the gunner, who would normally operate it with his right hand.

. . . The traversing hand-wheel is 10 1/2 inches in diameter and is situated in front of and above the level of the gunner's seat. The wheel is mounted horizontally with the handle on the underside. A plunger-type latch is pivoted to the handle and must be released before either the gunner or the commander can use their respective hand-wheels.

. . . The [gunner's] hydraulic power traverse system is controlled by a rocking footplate on the floor in front of the gunner's seat. The footplate is pivoted along the transverse axis. In the neutral position, the plate is tilted lower at the front than the back. On left traverse, the heel end of the plate is depressed until the plate is horizontal. On right traverse, the toe end of the plate is depressed to an angle of 24 degrees from the horizontal.

. . . The main armament is fired electrically by a curved steel bar pivoted on to the shaft of the elevating wheel. The bar can be operated by one finger but the gunner must first of all release the wheel handles, unless the latter is at the top centre of its arc of operation. The [coaxial] machine gun is operated by the gunner's right foot.

According to Tiger E tank gunner, Berent Isenberg, he seldom used his power traverse system, as his tank was normally in a defensive position, with the engine off. The manually operated turret traverse hand-wheel was his normal method of acquiring targets to his front, in conjunction with his manually operated elevation hand-wheel.

Besides his optical sighting instruments, the only other exterior vision for the gunner was a vision slit in the turret wall to his left, protected by thick laminated ballistic glass. An improved vision slit for the gunner, with a wider field of view, appeared on new production Tiger E tanks beginning in August 1943. Tiger E crewmember Berent Isenberg does not recall ever using the gunner's vision slit.

LOADER

The Tiger E tank loader was located on the right side of the 88mm main gun. The breech of the weapon and the recoil guard divided the turret into two separate half-sections. The loader was also responsible for the loading and servicing of the coaxial 7.92mm machine gun mounted on his side of the turret.

A British army examination of a Tiger E tank loader's position concluded this about the mounting of the coaxial 7.92mm machine gun:

"The loader has great difficulty in loading the coaxial machine gun because it is mounted so near the main armament. This position is a very bad feature, since, as the machine gun cannot be reloaded quickly, belts can only be fired intermittently and targets appearing for only a few seconds are likely to be missed during reloading."

On early model Tiger E tanks, the only exterior vision for the loader was a vision slit located in the turret wall to his right protected by thick laminated ballistic glass. An improved version of the vision slit appeared on production vehicles in August 1943, which provided a slightly wider field of view. Beginning in March 1943, all new-production Tiger E tanks boasted a fixed overhead periscope for the loader's position.

A Tiger E tank loader is cradling an 8.8cm round in his arms as he inserts it into the breech. Because an intercom cord would restrict the loader as he moved around to access the ammo stored in racks distributed throughout the fighting compartment, he did not wear a headset. Instead, he depended on verbal commands or hand signals from the commander or gunner to tell him what type of rounds to load. *Private collection*

A British army report describes the loader's position:

For the first time, the Germans have in this tank seriously considered the seating and comfort of the loader. His seat is mounted on the offside [right] of the fighting chamber, 22 1/2 inches above the turret platform. It is pivotally mounted on the elevation gearbox and normally faces to the rear. When not in use, however, it may be lifted and swung forwards under the gun. It is not adjustable for height.

From the loader's position inside a Tiger E tank, the breech housing of the 88mm main gun is clearly visible. The loader would insert a round into the circular opening of the breech housing when the breechblock (not seen here) was in the open position. Once the round is loaded, the breechblock closes automatically. *Tank Museum, Bovington*

Another British army report describes the manner in which the loader entered and left the Tiger E tank:

The loader's [overhead] hatch is rectangular and the door is hinged at the front. . . . The door falls flat on the turret roof when opened and does not increase the height of the tank. The loader must expose himself when opening it from inside the turret. An escape hatch is provided in the right rear quarter of the turret wall. It is circular and the door is hinged at the bottom and drops outward. Neither opening nor closing is spring-assisted, and once the door is opened, it is too heavy to be closed from inside the turret. In addition, when the door is open, it fouls the hull as the turret is being traversed. Since the loader would not leave the turret when the tank was in action, it appears that the hatch is used solely for escape in emergency, and that empty [cartridge] cases would be flung through the loader's roof hatch.

A Tiger E tank battalion report describes the various uses of the rear turret escape hatch on the vehicle:

The hatch is not only there for egress when in great danger, but also for the evacuation of the wounded, for establishing contact with nearby infantry, for tossing out spent cartridge cases, and for extinguishing engine compartment fires in battle from the hatch by traversing the turret to the three o'clock position. It is also used for egress to conduct the work needed for towing disabled tanks in battle.

A turret basket underneath the Tiger E tank turret attached to the turret ring with three pillars. All three crewmen in the vehicle's turret had seats attached to the turret ring, although the loader had to stand on the turret basket floorboard in order to load the main gun and to load and service the coaxial 7.92mm machine gun. A portion of the turret basket floorboard would fold up to allow access to the six main gun rounds stored there and other components.

DRIVER

In battle, tank drivers are continuously looking for firing positions that also afford protection from

Taken from the loader's position (looking rearward) is this view of the right side of the recoil guard. Also visible is the sheet metal guard that protects the commander from any main gun back-blast when the breech opens. Visible at the rear portion of the recoil guard is a pad that the spent main gun cartridge cases strike on ejection from the main gun upon counter-recoil. *Tank Museum, Bovington*

The Tiger E turret basket features a canvas sack attached to the recoil guard to catch empty cartridge cases as they are ejected. The stanchion sloping down from the elevating gearbox on the right of the gun passes under the gun to carry the gunner's seat on the left side of the gun. *Tank Museum, Bovington*

enemy observation and fire. They must always be prepared to bring the vehicle to a gradual halt to allow firing of the main gun. The driver must also smoothly drive the tank when the vehicle's machine guns are in use against stationary targets. Tank drivers also aid the tank commander and gunner in acquiring targets and observing the fall of the projectile to make trajectory corrections.

In his memoirs, Otto Carius describes the importance of the driver:

> Obviously, the greatest responsibility for the readiness of the tank fell to the driver. The man really had to be top notch. He had to drive using his head and not his "rear end." If he was on his toes, then his "Tiger" never left him in the lurch. The really good tank driver—and no other type was let loose on a "Tiger"—also had to have an instinctive feel for the terrain. He had to move properly cross-country. He always had to keep the tank's best side facing the enemy without the tank commander giving him every move first. Only then was it possible for a tank commander to concentrate completely on the enemy at hand. Only then could a platoon leader or company commander properly direct his vehicles in an operation without having to pay constant attention to the terrain.

The tank driver position also demanded a generous helping of guts. He was the only man in the vehicle who saw a lot yet had to remain completely passive when the tank was under fire and the rest of the crew slugged it out with the enemy. In those instances, he helped by observing and had to rely completely on his comrades in the turret.

A British army report describes the driver's position in the Tiger E tank:

> The driver sits in the front left corner of the hull. The seat is padded and is adjustable for forward-backward movement. The backrest is padded and hinged to the seat. Its angle of tilt is adjustable and the backrest can be dropped back flat to allow the driver easy access to the turret. The driver's legs are hemmed in uncomfortably between the steering band [final drive] castings. Since the height of the seat is non-adjustable, the driver has no "opened-up" position.
>
> The driver's main vision device is a visor, protected by a laminated glass block approximately 10 inches wide and three inches high, and mounted in the hull front plate. The block can be partly or wholly obscured by an exterior sliding shutter, which is adjusted by a hand-wheel on the mounting. The angle of view is satisfactory only when the shutter is fully open. In addition to the glass block, an episcope [periscope] is mounted in the driver's roof hatch door and faces half-left.

In addition to the driver's visor, early versions of the Tiger E tank included twin driver's periscopes designated the KFF2, directly above the driver's visor in the front vertical hull plate. Their 65-degree field of view allowed the driver to operate the vehicle with the visor closed. The periscopes disappeared from production vehicles beginning in February 1943. Those hulls that showed up with the two openings for the periscopes still drilled out had welded plugs inserted in their place.

In many tank designs, the driver's overhead hatch is directly above his seat, so he may operate the vehicle opened up, with his head and upper torso projected out over the top of the tank's hull roof. The designers of the Tiger E tank did not see that as necessary and made no provisions for that ability, and in fact, the driver's overhead hatch on the Tiger E tank (as well as the radioman's overhead hatch) is off-set a bit, to either side of the tank's front hull. This fact did not hinder Tiger E tank drivers from hanging out through their overhead turret hatches whenever a camera was present, as seen in some wartime German newsreels and pictures.

RADIOMAN

The radioman sat in the right front corner of the Tiger E tank hull and had an overhead circular armored hatch, nineteen inches in diameter, as did the driver. Both hatches hinged at the outside edge and were spring balanced, with a catch to lock them in a half-opened position. Unlike the driver's seat, the radioman's seat was not adjustable. However, the seat's backrest lifted out of the way to allow him to exit the vehicle by way of the turret if the need arose.

The short-range amplitude modulated (AM) voice radio in the standard Tiger E tank sat on top of the transmission housing that divided the radioman's position from the driver's position. The radio antenna was located on the right rear of the hull. Platoon leaders or company headquarters tanks had an extra radio that also mounted on top of the tank's transmission housing. Command versions of the Tiger E tank had two antennas on the rear hull and one on the turret.

Colonel Rock Marcone, U.S. Army (retired), who oversaw the largest tank battle that occurred during the opening stages of Operation Iraqi Freedom (OIF) in the summer of 2003, recounts his impressions on visiting the restored Tiger E tank belonging to the Tank Museum located at Bovington, England:

> Having been a keen student of military history most of my life, I always imagined the Tiger I tank being this massive machine. However, at first glance, I quickly realized that the U.S. Army's Abrams tank chassis is about five feet longer than the Tiger I. While the height on the two vehicles is about the same, the Abrams looks wider than the Tiger because the Abrams turret, looking face on, extends almost over the full width of the hull, while the turret on the Tiger presents a much narrower profile. The Abrams turret extends back over the engine deck area, much like that on the Tiger II tank.
>
> After seeing the Tiger tank up close, there are a number of similarities and differences between it and the Abrams tanks that caught my attention, the most obvious is the fact that the tank commander and gunner on the Tiger tank are on the left and the loader [is] on the right. This is just the opposite of the Abrams and all other American tanks before it,

The mounting bracket for the coaxially mounted 7.92mm machine gun (not fitted in this picture) is visible on the loader's side of this Tiger E tank. Also visible is the elevating arc and elevating pinion for raising and lowering the tank's main gun, as well as the loader's seat. *Tank Museum, Bovington*

> going back to the Sherman tank. Why they did this escapes me, the handling of the ammunition and storage had to be harder in the Tiger than the Abrams, since the Tiger loader had to use his left hand to push the round into the gun breech, rather than [his] right hand, as do our loaders.

TIGER B TANK DESCRIPTION

As early as May 1942, one month after the first prototypes of what would go on to become the Tiger E tank appeared before Hitler, a decision went into effect to start the ball rolling on the next generation German army heavy tank, with thicker armor and a longer and more powerful 88mm gun than that mounted on the Tiger E tank. The official German army Ordnance Department designation for the new heavy tank appeared in March 1943 as the Panzer Tiger (8.8cm KwK L/71) (SdKfz 182). In June 1943, it also acquired the designation Panzer Tiger Ausf. B, which was often shortened to just Tiger B.

The American and British armies had numerous designations and names for the Tiger B tank, which included the Mark VI, the Tiger II, the Royal Tiger, or the occasionally used unofficial German name, *Konigstiger,* which translates in English to "King Tiger."

Two command Tiger B tank variants were designated Tiger B *Panzerbefehelswagen* SdKfz 267 and SdKfz 268: one featured a radio arrangement to communicate with ground support aircraft and the other with higher headquarters out of the range of the standard tank-mounted radio sets. To make room for the additional radio sets in the command versions of the Tiger B tanks, they carried fewer main gun rounds than the standard production vehicle. Like the Tiger E command tanks, the Tiger B command tank sported additional antennas on the vehicle's hulls and turrets.

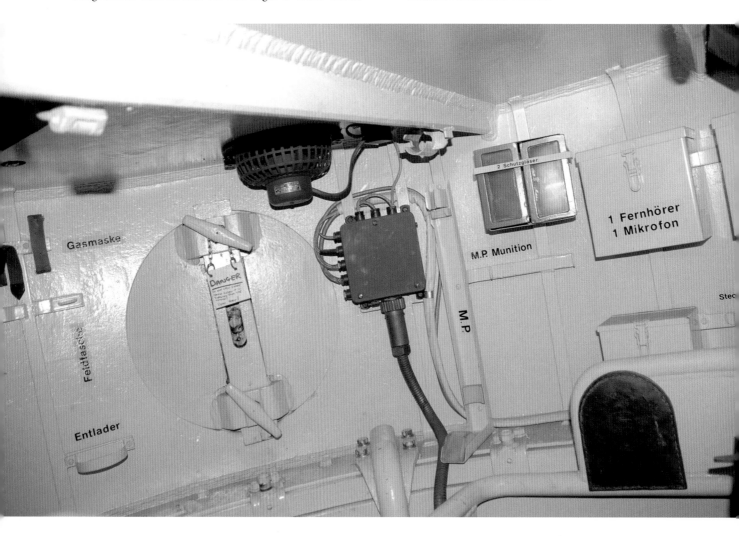

Looking rearward from the gunner's position on a Tiger E tank, the loader's escape hatch is visible. Overhead is the bottom portion of an electrically powered ventilation fan, with the upper portion projecting out over the top of the turret roof under an armored housing. *Tank Museum, Bovington*

The armor visor on the Tiger E tank was a serious ballistic weak spot in the tank's forward armor array. The thick ballistic glass block behind the visor could easily shatter with impacts from small-caliber projectiles. While the glass vision blocks were replaceable, they could also be jammed in place by enemy fire. *Vladimir Yakubov*

As with the Tiger E tank, the final contenders for the Tiger B tank chassis contract turned out to be Porsche and Henschel. Krupp once again received the contract to design and build the turret for the winning vehicle. The supremely confident Dr. Porsche once again began ordering components too early. Porsche had Krupp build fifty turrets before the contract decision came about. Much to his dismay, the Henschel vehicle proved to be the superior product once again and won the competition.

Preproduction of the Tiger B tank at Henschel's plant started in December 1943 with three evaluation vehicles. The first three Henschel series production units, with their Krupp turrets, came off the assembly line the next month. Of the original 1,500 units ordered, only 489 made it into service before the factories making them fell into Allied hands in March 1945. German army mismanagement of the Tiger B tank program and Allied bomber raids on the factories and transportation systems that fed the components to build the vehicles all played their part in the small numbers of the Tiger B tanks built.

The fifty Krupp turrets ordered by Porsche for his proposed version of the Tiger B tank appeared on the first fifty Henschel Tiger B production vehicles after being suitably modified. A superior turret designed and built by Krupp for the Henschel chassis subsequently appeared on their production vehicles, starting with the fifty-first unit built. The Germans referred to it as the *Serienturm,* "production series turret" in English.

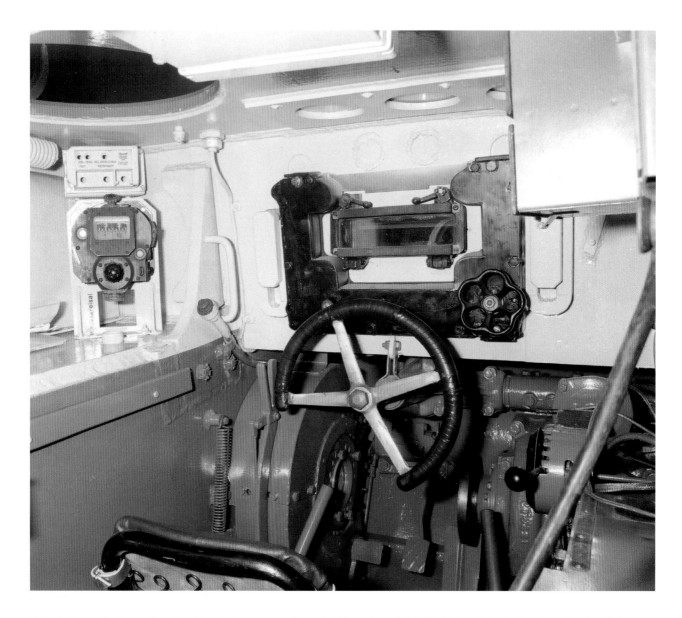

This photograph shows the driver's position in an early model Tiger E tank. Visible is the driver's steering wheel and the small circular handle used to open and close the driver's armor shutter for his direct-view vision port. To the driver's left is an electrically operated gyroscopic direction indicator (compass). *Tank Museum, Bovington*

A U.S. Army technical intelligence report, based on a British army supplied report, provided a description of a Tiger B tank based on battlefield observations. The report dates from August 1944.

A preliminary report as yet unchecked has been received on a 67-ton redesigned Tiger tank mounting an 8.8cm KwK 43 gun. The general appearance of this equipment is that of a scaled up Panther and it conforms to normal German tank practice in so far as the design, layout, the interlocking

of the main plates and the welding are concerned. The engine is in the rear and the gearbox [transmission] and the steering and driving units are in front.

A second U.S. Army report, dated September 13, 1944, and based on British army information, provides more information on the Tiger B tank:

A badly damaged specimen of the new redesigned Tiger tank, mounting the 8.8cm KwK 43 L/71 gun,

SdKfz182, has been examined in the British Sector in Normandy. This tank bears little resemblance to the previous Tiger tank, first encountered in North Africa, but has many features in common with the Panther, particularly as regards [to] the sloping of the main armour plates. However, it would be a mistake to compare it with any previous German tank, as it mounts a gun with a much superior performance to the gun in either the previous Tiger or Panther tanks and its armour affords a much greater degree of protection. Thickest armour is 150mm (5.9 inches) on the glacis plate, which is sloped at 40 degrees from the vertical. Semi-official names, which have been used for this tank, are Tiger II and *Konigstiger* (Royal Tiger).

The report went on to list the vehicle as being twenty-three feet ten inches long excluding the main gun and thirty-two feet eight inches long with the main gun pointed directly over the front of the hull. With the mud flaps fitted, the Tiger B tank was eleven feet eleven inches wide. The tank was ten feet two inches tall.

A postwar British army report on an early production Tiger B tank goes into detail on certain aspects of the crew positions. The first passage describes the tank commander's position:

> The commander's station is in the left rear quarter of the turret. He has three alternative positions: first, seated in the seat, secondly, standing on the footrests, and thirdly, standing on the turret floor. The seat is saddle-shaped and the top is 11 inches long and a foot and a 1/2-inch wide and covered with imitation leather. It is mounted on a hinged arm on the turret wall and can be stowed against it when not required. No other adjustment is provided. The backrest is also covered with imitation leather and is 11 inches wide and four inches high. It is hinged and can, like the seat, be stowed against the turret wall when not required.

Another passage from the same British army report describes the detail of the gunner's power traverse system for the tank's turret and their impressions of it.

> The [gunner's] traverse hand-wheel is very badly positioned. When the gunner is seated, the linkage between the wheel and the gearing is between his

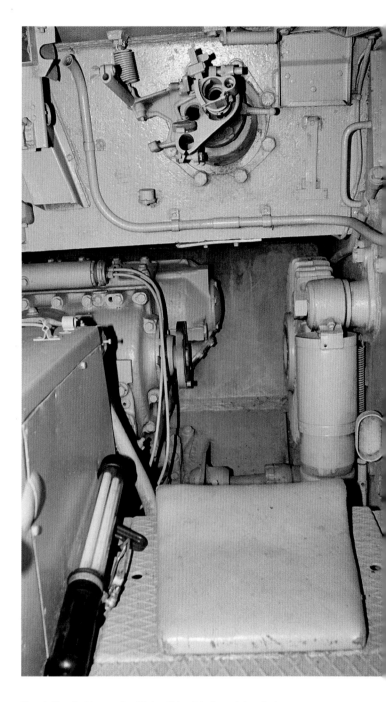

From the bottom of a Tiger E tank's turret basket can be seen the radioman's position. Visible is the mounting bracket for a 7.92mm machine gun. To the left of the radioman's seat pad is the transmission housing. The radios normally installed on the top of the transmission housing are long gone from this vehicle, as is the drive shaft, which formerly connected the right final drive to the transmission. *Andreas Kirchoff*

Like the Panther medium tank, the Tiger B tank featured heavily sloped upper and lower glacis front hull plates, whose thickness and slope provided an exceptional level of armor protection from Allied tank and tank guns. Befitting its great weight, the tank appeared with wide tracks to allow the vehicle to cross soft ground without sinking. *David Marian*

knees, which must be kept apart. In such a cramped station, the gunner would soon become very uncomfortable and probably fatigued. . . .

Fortunately, for the gunner, the turret can also be traversed by power. There are two controls which can be used either independently or, as is more likely, together. The first control is a tilting floor-plate, which is set into the floor in front of the gunner's seat. The plate is one foot one inch long from front to back and one foot wide and is pivoted along its length. It can be locked in the neutral position when not required.

The axis of the plate is mounted approximately six inches to the right of the centre of the gunner's seat, and traversing is difficult in either direction. On left traverse, the gunner's left foot depresses the left half of the plate; this is awkward because the gunner's left leg jams against the traverse hand-wheel spindle. On right traverse, the side of the gunner's right boot scrapes against the side of the hole cut into the turret floor and his boot tends to slip off the plate. The plate inspected was stiff to operate independently though when used in conjunction with the hand lever, it proved more satisfactory.

A Tiger B tank shows the long overhang of the rear turret bustle, which not only acted as a counterweight for the long and heavy main gun, but as additional storage space for main gun rounds. This particular example lacks the typical external storage features seen on wartime vehicles. It does feature the typical twin curved engine exhaust pipes on the rear hull plate. *Andreas Kirchoff*

The [gunner's] hand lever is a plain steel bar mounted on the left side of the seat. The bar is operated by moving it either forwards (left traverse) or backwards (right traverse), and it is mounted on the same linkage as the footplate. When the bar is pulled backwards, the gunner's left elbow tends to strike the commander's left footrest. Although more satisfactory than just a foot-pedal, the combination of foot-pedal and hand lever is still, in our opinion, not as efficient as the spade-grip type of control.

Like the gunner on the Tiger E tank, the Tiger B tank gunner fired the main gun electrically. The trigger for the main gun on the Tiger B tank consisted of a steel bar hinged to the shaft cover of the elevating wheel, located next to the gunner's right hand, the bar being curved and lying parallel to the rim of the elevating wheel.

Unlike the positions of the tank commander and the gunner on the Tiger B tank, the British army evaluation of the same tank found the loader's position on the vehicle to be more satisfactory.

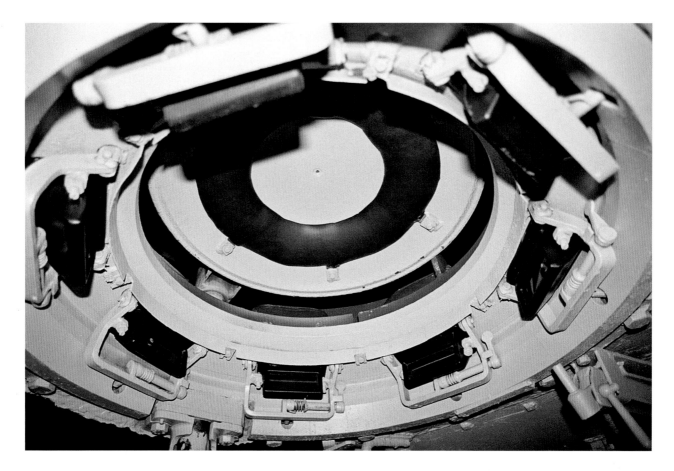

From inside a Tiger B tank can be seen the interior of the tank commander's cupola. Visible are the periscopes that provided the vehicle commander with his exterior vision. Because tanks often provide a rough ride when off-road, there is padding around the bottom of the slightly open tank commander's hatch. *Michael Green*

The loader has ample space for handling ammunition on his side of the turret. In addition, if his hatch is open, a loader whose height is five feet seven inches or less can stand erect with his head not touching the turret roof. However, when the hatch is closed, the fitting on the inside of the door projects about three inches below the level of the roof. Since the loader would probably strike his head against it when loading he would probably keep the hatch door open when loading. An auxiliary traverse hand-wheel is provided for the loader so that he can assist the gunner to traverse the turret when the power traverse mechanism is not being used. A latch on the gunner's wheel prevents the loader from operating his wheel independently.

The report goes on to describe the steering controls for the Tiger B tank driver and the various foot-operated pedals:

Since the [driver's] seat is adjustable for upper and lower positions, the controls have been designed to be accessible when the driver is in either position. Power-assisted steering is controlled by a semi-circular wheel one foot three inches in diameter. The wheel column is jointed and the wheel can be raised or lowered to suit the driver's position. The wheel column is also telescopic and can be extended through 11 inches as required. In general, the wheel is very satisfactory and more comfortable to use than the orthodox steering levers fitted in most armored fighting vehicles. A disadvantage, however, is that the wheel is effective only for power-assisted steering. If the power system is not running (e.g., when the vehicle is being towed), the usual manual steering is used. This is controlled by two standard steering levers, each one foot nine and a half inches long, mounted on the hull floor,

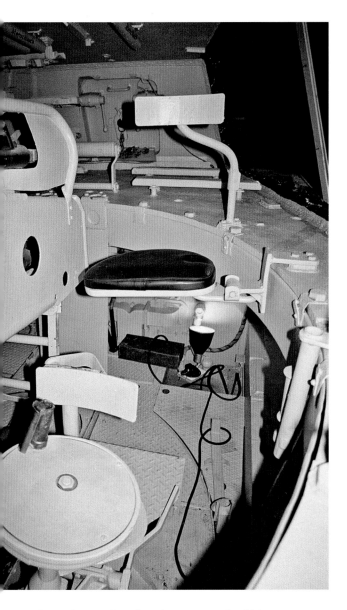

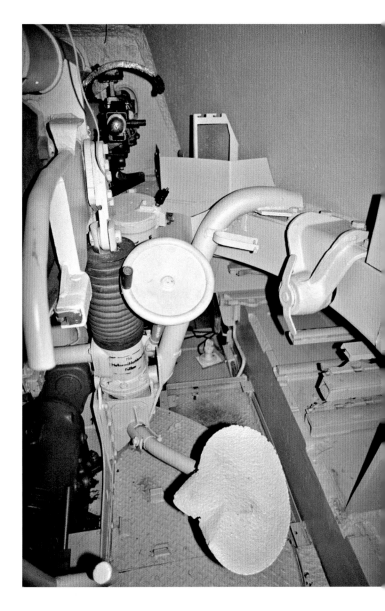

Seats for the Tiger B tank gunner and vehicle commander are visible in this picture. Clearly visible in the foreground is the manually operated traversing hand-wheel for the gunner who sits below and in front of the commander. Both the commander's seat bottom and backrest fold to one side when not required. *Michael Green*

The Tiger B tank loader's seat is visible in this picture as is his manually operated turret traverse hand-wheel. The loader's hand-wheel gave the gunner much-needed assistance when manually traversing the large and heavy turret. At the top of the picture is the coaxially mounted 7.92mm machine gun. At the middle right of the photograph is a turret locking handle. *Michael Green*

one on each side of the driver's legs. The levers are accessible only when the driver is in his lower position, and valuable space is required for two sets of steering controls. The driver's hand is liable to catch on the gearbox direction lever as he pulls back the right steering lever.

The Tiger B driver could drive "opened up" with his head and upper torso projecting out over the superstructure roof. The tank designers provided the Tiger B driver with two accelerator pedals at different heights, as explained in a British army report. Also described are the vision arrangements of the Tiger B tank and the British evaluation of them.

Two separate accelerator pedals are provided. The lower control is a plate three and a 1/2 inches wide and 10 and 3/4 inches long, which is riveted to the floor. The pedal is almost vertical and consequently difficult to operate. The upper control is a roller four inches long and one and 1/2 inches wide mounted on a common linkage with the lower pedal. A hinged plate four and 1/2 inches wide, which can be folded when not in use, is fitted as a footrest. The pedal is rather difficult to find with the foot but is otherwise satisfactory.

When driving "opened-up" the driver has an adequate vision range, since his head and shoulders are outside the hull of the tank. When the vehicle is being driven "closed-down" his sole vision device is a five-inch wide episcope [periscope]. A handle on each side of its mounting is used to control the episcope's angle of tilt and rotation. Although the driver can see the ground from six yards onwards in front of the vehicle, the fitting of only one episcope for the driver of so large a tank is bad. The vision range with the episcope is so restricted that, probably, even an experienced driver would have to rely on his commander's instructions when driving "closed-down" along a narrow or devious route. This is undesirable, as the commander should at all times be free to look for targets, instead of concentrating on whether or not the driver is keeping the correct course.

Early on in the design of what would go on to become the Tiger B tank, it was envisioned that a crew hatch be located in either the rear of the vehicle's turret or on one side of the tank's turret. As design work on the turret for the Tiger B tank progressed, the hatch showed

Looking directly down on the gunner's position in a Tiger B tank, the large manually operated traversing hand-wheel is visible, as is the smaller manually operated elevation hand-wheel to its right. Behind the elevation hand-wheel is the firing handle for the main gun pulled toward the gunner for firing. *Michael Green*

Looking up from the loader's position in a Tiger B tank is the complicated mechanism of his overhead hatch. Such needlessly overengineered mechanisms contributed to the cost and complexity of wartime production. To the left of the hatch is the bottom portion of an electrically powered ventilation fan with the upper portion projecting out over the top of the turret roof under an armored housing. *Michael Green*

up in design drawings at the rear of the turret. In this location, it allowed for the installing or removing of the 88cm main gun and its mount, if necessary.

The British army decided, based on examinations of captured Tiger B tanks, that the rear turret hatch was primarily an escape hatch for the vehicle's crew, as seen in this passage from one of their reports.

> A turret escape hatch is fitted into the rear wall of the turret and is one foot eight inches wide and one foot two inches high. When the turret bulge [bustle] ammunition bins are full, the rounds project around and beneath the hatch, making evacuation almost impossible, even for a slim crewmember. When the bins are emptied (a situation [that] would be operationally dangerous) the hatch is more accessible, but can still be used only by a very thin man. In emergency, the crewmembers would probably prefer to risk getting out with the smoke through the roof hatches rather than chance being caught in the escape hatch or one of the many projections surrounding it.

The designers of the Tiger B rear hatch must have been counting on some member of the turret crew accessing the rear turret hatch as they installed a pistol port in it that closed with an armored plug.

TIGER TANK MOBILITY

A good tank design is a balance of firepower, protection, mobility, and reliability. Firepower and protection of both Tiger variants is legendary. Their mobility and reliability, however, constituted the weaker aspects of these tanks. Mobility breaks down into three classes, with transport into a zone of operation being strategic mobility and the ability to move rapidly around a zone of operation (once it has gotten there) being operational mobility. There is also tactical mobility, the ability to move quickly to firing positions and evade enemy fire. Reliability usually includes not only robustness of the mechanical design but also ease of repair or replacement of components. The Achilles' Heel of the Tigers, their propulsion systems, includes the engine, transmission, track drives, suspension system, road wheels, and tracks.

TIGER TANK ENGINES

Various models of Maybach liquid-cooled, gasoline-powered aircraft engines, specially modified for tank usage, propelled almost all World War II German tanks. American tanks used both air-cooled and liquid-cooled gasoline and diesel engines, as did the British Commonwealth forces. Russian medium and heavy tanks employed during World War II were all liquid-cooled diesel engines.

The selection of Maybach engines had less to do with the merits of the firm's products than it did with the

A picture from the rear of a Tiger B tank turret shows the tank commander's cupola, the loader's hatch, and the upper portion of the electrically powered ventilation turret fan. The smaller feature on the turret centerline is a port through which the loader disposed of spent main gun cartridge cases. *Andreas Kirchoff*

close personal relationship between the head of the company and Adolph Hitler. This cronyism did much to hamstring German tank designs before and during World War II.

In both versions of the Tiger tank, the roughly 2,860-pound engine was centrally located at the rear of the hull with the flywheel end forward. A large overhead armored rectangular hatch on the vehicles provided access to their engines. There was also an automatic fire extinguisher system installed in the engine compartments of both Tiger tanks.

The large radiators that resided on either side of the engine compartment, for both versions of the Tiger tanks, received overhead protection for both their air intake and exhaust output from heavy armored grilled plates. Engine torque in the Tiger tanks was transmitted to the transmission located in between the driver and the radioman through a driveshaft under the turret floor.

Tiger tank engines started with a 24-volt electric starter or with an inertia starter that operated with either a hand crank or an external starter motor. The Tiger B tank also featured a small gasoline engine for use as a backup starter motor.

Both versions of the Tiger tank had two batteries located beneath the hull floor, forward of the engine firewall. The two batteries connected in series to operate the tank's 24-volt electric starter motors. A generator in the tank provided power for the vehicle's electrical system and charged the batteries when the tank's engine was running.

The first 250 production Tiger E tanks had V-12 1,302-cubic-inch engines, designated HL210 P45, rated at 650 horsepower (hp) at 3,000 revolutions per minute (rpm). However, frequent engine failures in service resulted in the governed speed lowered to 2,500 rpm. Because of this limitation, the Tiger E tank found itself considered underpowered by many.

At the very rear of the Tiger B tank bustle was a large crew hatch that also provided a path to install or remove the vehicle's main gun. Missing from this picture are the large main gun rounds stored in the ammunition racks seen on either side of the turret bustle, which must have made it very difficult to leave by this exit if those racks were full. *Michael Green*

Part of the problem with the Maybach HL210 P45 engine not meeting its power requirements was the very short eight-month development time. This left little time for testing the engine to uncover any shortcomings in its design before production commenced.

Despite its lack of sufficient horsepower for the Tiger E tank, the Maybach HL210 P45 engine was a marvel of engineering for its time. It was only four feet long, three feet two inches wide, and three feet one inch tall. The British army examined the Maybach engine from a Tiger E tank captured in North Africa and was impressed with its compactness, finish, and workmanship in comparison to their own tank engines.

The HL210 engine was upgraded to 700 horsepower and was redesignated as the HL230 P45, starting with Tiger E tank hull 251 in May 1943. They replaced the original aluminum cylinder block with a cast-iron cylinder block, which allowed them to increase the displacement by almost 12 percent to 1,457 cubic inches. This engine powered late production Tiger E tanks, and HL230 variants powered both the Panther medium tank series and the Tiger B tank.

Like its predecessor, though, the HL230 engine lacked the durability to run for long periods at rated speed. To prolong engine service life, the builders had the engine de-rated to 650 horsepower in November 1943 by reducing the governed speed to 2,500 rpm,

This is an exterior view of the rear turret crew hatch on a Tiger B tank fitted with a Krupp/Henschel turret. The rear turret crew hatch exterior arrangement differed on those Tiger B tanks fitted with the Krupp/Porsche turret. With both turret designs, the rear turret crew hatch hinged downward. The hatch pictured is missing the plug for the pistol port opening. *Andreas Kirchoff*

making the heavier Tiger B tank even more underpowered than the Tiger E tank.

HORSEPOWER PER TON AND ITS IMPORTANCE

Engine power divided by gross vehicle weight (horsepower per ton) is a relatively accurate measure of mobility performance. The gross power to weight ratio of early 650 horsepower Tiger E tanks was 11.5 horsepower per ton. The 700 horsepower upgrade raised this to 12.5 gross horsepower per ton. In comparison, World

War I tanks averaged between four to five gross horsepower per ton.

The U.S. Army M4A3 Sherman medium tank weighed about thirty-four tons and received power from a Ford liquid-cooled, 500-horsepower, gasoline engine (14.5 gross horsepower per ton). The heavier Sherman replacement, the forty-six-ton M26 Pershing medium tank with the same Ford 500-horsepower engine, reduced the power to weight ratio to 10.8 gross horsepower per ton. The relatively low power ratio of the Pershing was compensated for in some respects by its

The driver's position on a Tiger B tank with the steering wheel and the large transmission housing, which separated the driver from the radioman, located on the other side of it. Also seen in this picture is the shift control unit for the driver and the two backup steering levers on either side of his seat. *Michael Green*

automatic transmission, which allowed continuous flow of power without interruptions due to gear shifting.

The 1,500-horsepower, sixty-ton M1 Abrams tank was the first U.S. Army tank with 25 gross horsepower per ton. The 1,500 horsepower diesel engine in the fifty-four-ton German army Leopard 2A5 tank provides 27 gross horsepower per ton, while the most recent tank designed for the Japanese Self-Defense Force provides 30 gross horsepower per ton.

TIGER TANK TRANSMISSIONS

A problem with all tracked vehicles has to do with the conflicting demands placed on them. High tractive efforts, such as climbing a slope, requires high sprocket torques at low speed, while high-speed travel on level ground requires higher rpms, albeit at lower torque. Because engines cannot develop these torque/speed extremes and because they operate at optimal efficiency over only a very small torque/speed range, it is the transmission's job to match a vehicle's speed and torque requirements to the most efficient speed and torque range of an engine. In tracked vehicles, transmissions provide a very large range of output torques while keeping the engine speed and torque relatively constant.

The Tiger E tank featured a Maybach-designed, hydraulically operated, semi-automatic transmission designated Olvar 40 12 16. The Tiger B tank was equipped

with a reconfigured version designated Olvar 40 12 16 Ausf. B (model B). Both versions provided eight forward and four reverse gear ratios. Mechanical power from the rear-mounted Tiger E and Tiger B engine traveled to the transmission through a driveshaft that ran underneath the turret basket floor. The gearshift lever in both versions of the Tiger tanks was located to the driver's right and mounted on the side of the transmission housing.

Tiger transmissions were semi-automatic. This means that the drivers were not required to use the clutch to manually disengage the drive train for every gear change. Clutching was required to start the vehicle and to switch between forward and reverse. Hydraulically activated clutches in the transmission eliminated the need for manual clutching by the driver.

According to a Tiger B tank driver's manual, with the engine running at its top governed speed of 2,500 rpm, the vehicle in first gear could reach 1.24 miles per hour (mph). Second gear was capable of 1.9 mph. The transmission would be in sixth gear at 10 mph and in eighth gear at the top speed of 21 mph. In reverse, the Tiger B tank could reach a top speed of 5.6 mph in fourth gear.

STEERING GEAR

Most tanks are equipped with a laterally rigid pair of tracks. In order to steer them, the outside track in a turn

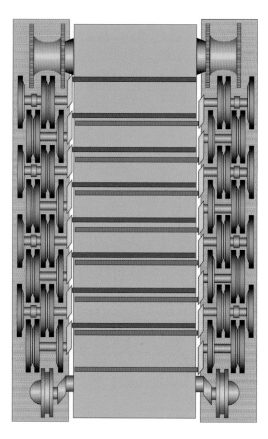

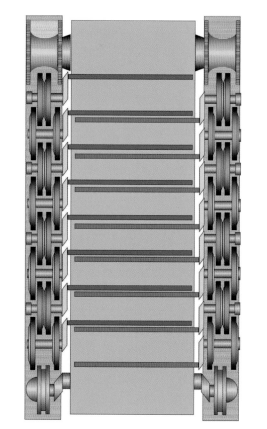

The large number of road wheels on the Tiger E tank and their interleaved arrangement was the designer's attempt to deal with the increasing weight of the vehicle as it progressed from the planning stage to series production vehicle. This illustration shows which road wheels came off the vehicle when being shipped by rail. *James D. Brown*

must move faster than the inside track. Steering mechanisms typically form part of a tank's transmission, as it did with the Tiger tanks, and transmit power to a tank's final drives located on either side of the front or rear hull.

The Tiger tanks had their final drives located at the very front of their hulls. Attached to the exterior of the Tiger tank's final drives were the drive sprockets that turned the tank's tracks. Track return idlers at the rear served to contain the end of the tracks opposite the drive sprockets.

Due to the weight of the Tiger E tank, the German firm of Henschel decided to adopt a double differential steering system for the vehicle and designated it the L 600. For the Tiger B tank, Henschel used a modified version of the L 600 and assigned it the designation L 801. Henschel went with the double differential steering system because the company felt that the other types of steering systems

then available lacked the durability and strength to turn a vehicle as large and heavy as the Tiger E tank.

Unlike automobiles and modern tanks, whose turning radii are continuously variable and proportional to a driver's control input, a double differential has only two turn radii for each gear ratio. The double differential steering system thus provided the Tiger tank driver with two different turning radii for each of the eight forward and four reverse transmission gear ratios. The direction he chose to turn his tank and the speed of the turns were dependent on the engagement of four hydraulically operated multi-disc clutches that the driver operated with a steering wheel.

The smallest turning radius on the Tiger E tank was about eleven feet and the maximum turning radius was 181 yards, while the Tiger B tank had a minimum turning

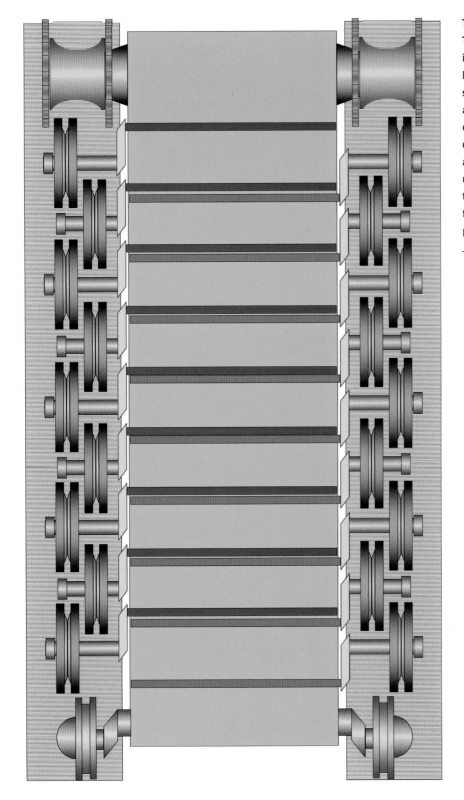

The overlapping road wheels of the Tiger B tank (shown here) were an improvement over the interleaved layout of the Tiger E tank but were still prone to jamming by mud, rocks, and ice and still required considerable effort to replace damaged inner road wheels. This arrangement also induced undesirable twisting loads on the track pins as the road wheels shifted from side to side as the vehicle progressed over the track blocks.
James D. Brown

A vehicle restoration specialist at the Tank Museum, located in Bovington, England, is inserting a high-hardness steel torsion bar into the hull of the Tiger E tank. It will run across the bottom of the vehicle's hull to an anchor on the opposite side of the hull.
Tank Museum, Bovington

radius of about seven feet and a maximum turning radius of 125 yards.

With the Tiger tank transmission in neutral, the driver could perform a 360-degree pivot or neutral turn, in which the two tracks moved in opposite directions at the same speed. An American tank officer commented on the neutral steering ability of the German Panther and Tiger tanks compared to his M4 series Sherman tank, in a March 1945 U.S. Army report:

"The small turning radius when standing still is a desirable feature of the German tanks. Would like this feature incorporated in our own tanks."

As a backup emergency steering system, the Tiger tank drivers had brake steering levers mounted on either side of their seats, which allowed them to use a clutch and brake steering system to turn their vehicles. The Tiger tanks had mechanical disc brakes that were engaged by either the driver's brake pedal or the brake steering levels.

FUEL TANKS

Fuel for the Tiger E tank engine came from a number of containers described in a British army report:

"There are four petrol [fuel] tanks, two at each side of the engine compartment. The top tank in each side is of wedge shape and the lower is rectangular. The total capacity of the tanks is 125 gallons."

The maximum range of the Tiger E tank on level road was about 121 miles. Off-road range was 68 miles or less.

A U.S. Army report on the Tiger B tank stated that the vehicle had seven interconnected fuel tanks, which had a total capacity of 203 gallons. The fuel complement in the Tiger B tank provided a maximum range on level

roads of 106 miles. When traveling off-road, the range of the Tiger B tank dropped to around 74 miles.

SUSPENSION

A tank's ability to travel quickly over rough terrain is dependent both on engine power and the suspension system. The Tiger tanks used a mechanical suspension system consisting of numerous road arm stations on either side of the hull, with the road arms connected to transversely mounted high-hardness steel torsion bars that ran across the hull to anchors on the opposite side of the hull. Spindles fitted to the lower ends of the road arms accepted the road wheels for each arm.

As the Tiger tanks drove over rough terrain, the mass of the tank acting against the motion of the road arms caused the torsion bar springs to rotate. The twisting action of the torsion bars pushed the road wheels back down to keep them on the ground. Because the pure springing action of torsion bars alone would cause a vehicle to pitch uncontrollably even on relatively smooth terrain, four shock absorbers mounted on the front and rear suspension road arms controlled the tendency of the hull to resonate on the torsion-bar suspension. In physics, control over resonance is called damping. A rubber bumper at each shock absorber location cushioned occasional bottoming of the suspension.

The most notable external feature of the suspension system on the Tiger tanks was their use of a very large number of road wheels. The types of road wheels and their numbers varied on the Tiger E tank; originally they were equipped with 31.5-inch-diameter, inverted, dish-like steel road wheels (twenty-four on either side of the vehicle's hull) fitted with solid rubber rims. In February

Visible in this picture, taken from the turret basket of a Tiger E tank, is the large steel metal housing that contained the vehicle's transmission and divided the front hull in half, with the radioman on the right and the driver on the left. Visible just in front of the transmission is the steering unit. A large shock absorber appears on the driver's side of the transmission. *Andreas Kirchoff*

1944, in an effort to rationalize production and trim production time and cost, the Tiger E tank began coming off the production lines with 31.5-inch-diameter flat steel road wheels inherited from the Tiger B tank. Rather than being rimmed with solid rubber, the road wheels from the Tiger B tank were steel rimmed, cushioned by an interior layer of rubber. Due to the increased load-bearing capacity of the Tiger B tank road wheels, the number of road wheels on either side of the Tiger E tank dropped from twenty-four to sixteen, only two per road arm rather than the previous three per road arm. The Tiger B tank featured eighteen road wheels per hull side.

The number of road wheels and their diameter is one of the earliest design decisions made when laying out a new tank. Even though tank tracks spread vehicle weight more evenly than the wheels, there are still soil pressure distributions centered under the road wheels. If the soil bearing strength is exceeded under any road wheel, the soil will fail there and the track will sink, simultaneously decreasing tractive effort and increasing rolling resistance, a lose-lose situation. Maintaining tractive effort and minimizing sinkage would therefore seem to favor large numbers of road wheels to spread soil loads as evenly as possible.

There is a practical limit to the number of road wheels, however. The radii of the road wheels sets this

This photograph shows the transmission and steering unit coming out through the turretless hull of the Tiger E tank, belonging to the collection of the Tank Museum located at Bovington, England. At the bottom of the vehicle's hull can be seen some of the tank's torsion bars. *Tank Museum, Bovington*

limit. As the number of road wheels is increased, wheel radii must decrease to avoid interference. Herein lies the rub: rolling resistance of a cross-country vehicle increases as wheel diameter decreases. Our common experience allows us to contemplate a "dirt bike" optimized for off-road travel, but we will never see "dirt roller skates" because the inherent small wheel diameters of roller skates offers rolling resistance too high to be overcome.

The Tiger suspensions were an attempt to spread vehicle soil loads over as many road wheel stations as possible while retaining the lower rolling resistance of large road wheels. The compromise partially attained its intended goal, but at a cost of increased maintenance and lowered reliability.

In contrast to the interleaved road wheels of the Tiger E tank, the Tiger B tank had a nine-road-arm, overlapping wheel arrangement. The Tiger E interleaved road wheels were close together. This encouraged ice, rocks, mud, and

other objects to jam the wheels. While the overlapping road wheel arrangement on the Tiger B tank was an improvement, overlapping road wheels place a potentially damaging twisting load on tank tracks. In addition to these faults, both interleaved and overlapping road wheel configurations are heavier and more difficult to maintain than the more typical double road wheels found on other World War II tanks. Interleaved and overlapping road wheels never appeared on any other postwar production tank designs.

TRACKS

The Tiger E cast-manganese-steel tracks consisted of ninety-six track shoes connected by unlubricated removable steel pins. The 28.5-inch-wide service tracks had double guide horns and extended beyond the sides of the vehicle's hull.

The extreme width of the Tiger E tank with the service tracks fitted (twelve feet three inches) presented an obstacle for rail transport. Hence, narrower twenty-inch transport tracks went on the tank to prevent interference with railroad trackside structures. The transport tracks brought down the width of the Tiger E tank to just ten feet four inches. When fitted with the transport tracks, the outer road wheels came off, along with their hub extensions. Manuals indicated that a Tiger E tank crew should be able to change a single track in thirty minutes.

On the Tiger B tank, the two cast-manganese-steel service tracks were thirty-two inches wide and extended beyond the hull. Unlike the Tiger E tank side fenders, which were sheet metal, those on Tiger B tanks were armored and provided additional side protection to the suspension system. The total width of the vehicle was eleven feet eleven inches over the tracks (twelve feet eight inches including side skirts). The Tiger B tracks had double guide horns. The Tiger B tank also had twenty-six-inch-wide transport tracks, employed when being shipped by rail.

By way of comparison, the width of the first generation of U.S. Army M4 series Sherman tanks, without track extensions, was almost nine feet, while the second generation of M4 series Sherman tanks, without track extensions, was almost ten feet. The World War II U.S. Army M26 Pershing tank had a width of eleven and one-half feet, and the current M1 Abrams tank series has a width of twelve feet including its armor skirts.

Sitting on a stand in the vehicle restoration shop of the Tank Museum, located in Bovington, England, is the very compact, gasoline-powered, water-cooled engine for the Tiger E tank that belongs to the museum's very impressive collection. The engine is not the vehicle's original, but it came from a Tiger B tank in the collection. *Tank Museum, Bovington*

The Tiger B left and right track strings each consisted of ninety track shoes held together with unlubricated removable steel pins. The running surface of the tracks on both versions of the Tiger tank had chevron-pattern grousers cast into them for better grip with the ground.

With its turret turned to one side in order to gain access to the rear engine deck is an early model Tiger E tank. The length of the 8.8cm gun tube is evident in this picture. The gun tubes on pre–World War II German tanks did not extend past the front hull of the vehicles for ease of shipping. *David Marian*

The powerful 8.8cm main gun mounted in the turret of the Tiger E tank is about sixteen feet long and features a large muzzle brake at the end of the gun tube, which helps to retard the recoil of the weapon and keeps down the amount of dust kicked up when fired. *Andreas Kirchoff*

CHAPTER TWO
FIREPOWER

The Tiger tank turret-mounted 88mm (8.8cm) main guns went a long way in helping the Germans achieve their legendary status on the battlefields of World War II. While those guns now pale in comparison to the range and penetration abilities of modern tank main guns, in their time they were extremely potent weapons feared by any enemy that got within their effective range. British and American soldiers of World War II referred to any type of 8.8cm gun they met as the "88," while the typical German soldier called the guns "*Acht und Achtzig*," which translates to "eight and eighty."

The 8.8cm main guns carried by the Tiger tanks during World War II evolved from a prewar German military requirement for an effective antiaircraft gun. It was Krupp, the famous German arms-making company, working in secret with the Swedish firm of Bofors in the 1920s, that laid down the initial design parameters of what would become the basis of the dreaded 8.8cm antiaircraft/antitank gun. In 1931, Krupp design engineers convened in Essen, Germany. They completed the first 8.8cm antiaircraft gun prototype in early 1932. Their long years of careful development paid off, and the prototype gun greatly impressed the German military.

With the takeover of the German government by Adolf Hitler and the Nazi party in 1933, a massive rearmament program began, and the new Krupp 8.8cm antiaircraft gun entered into service the same year as the 8.8cm FlaK 18, L/56. The term *FlaK* is a German abbreviation for *Fliegerabwehr Kanone,* the English translation for *antiaircraft gun.* The L/56 referred to the 56-caliber length of the gun measured from the muzzle to the rear face of the breech ring.

The term *caliber* defines the bore diameter of a gun. In large guns, design nomenclature may also refer to barrel length as a multiple of the caliber, thus an 8.8cm L/56 denotes a gun with an 8.8cm bore diameter and a barrel $8.8 \times 56 = 492.8$ cm (sixteen feet) long. The designation 8.8cm L/56 is a much handier specification than 8.8cm L/492.8, so barrel length as a multiple of bore diameter is in almost universal use.

The bore of a weapon is that part of a gun barrel that provides a path for a projectile to travel. All World War II tank main guns featured rifled bores. Rifling consists of spiral grooves in the bore that spin a projectile as it travels down the barrel. A spinning projectile is more stable in flight, which makes the trajectory more predictable.

This German pre–World War II photograph shows the many men needed to operate the 8.8cm antiaircraft gun. The weapon, designed in the 1920s, did not enter into production until the 1930s. It first saw combat with the German military during the Spanish Civil War (1936–1939). *National Archives*

Most modern tank guns are smoothbore, and the projectiles are now fin-stabilized rather than spin-stabilized in flight.

The 8.8cm FlaK 18, L/56 started out with a barrel life of only nine hundred rounds. With the introduction of a new type of propellant, this increased to about three thousand rounds; even this number proved unsatisfactory to the German military, so a research program began in 1935 to increase barrel life. The solution came from Rheinmetall, Krupp's business rival. With their newly designed longer-lasting gun barrel, the Krupp 8.8cm L/56 gun became the 8.8cm FlaK 36, L/56 and

began entering service between 1936 and 1937. The 8.8cm FlaK 37, L/56 soon followed it into service.

Rheinmetall produced the 8.8cm FlaK 41, L/74—the last of the 8.8cm FlaK guns. They began entering into service in 1943 and were equally effective in both the antiaircraft and antitank roles. Due to a number of unresolved design issues, only a limited number entered service before the war in Europe ended in May 1945.

ANTITANK ROLE

The 8.8cm FlaK guns frequently found themselves pressed into an antitank role during the German

An American soldier looks at the destroyed remains of a German 8.8cm antiaircraft gun at the side of a French road. The weapon fired a twenty-one-pound projectile to an effective ceiling of about 26,000 feet. A well-trained 8.8cm gun crew could manually load and fire up to fifteen rounds per minute. *National Archives*

invasion of France in the summer of 1940. This was an unfamiliar role for the crews of the guns, who fitted them with ad-hoc armored shields for limited protection from small-arms fire and artillery fragments. The drawback of these shields was the loss of elevation for antiaircraft employment. A standard production shield soon appeared that permitted the use of the weapon at all elevations. The 8.8cm FlaK gun was large—about 7 feet tall, 9.5 feet wide, and 19 feet long. Their large size made them easy targets for high-explosive (HE) fire. Hence, German gun crews did their best to camouflage their positions from enemy observation.

British tankers first experienced the full might of the 8.8cm FlaK guns on May 20, 1940, during the battle

for France. A British tank attack on German units was decimated by artillery and 8.8cm FlaK guns pressed into the antitank role. The British lost thirty-six tanks that day, eight of them to the 8.8cm FlaK guns. Their success was well noted by the German military as a whole, and in particular by Gen. Erwin Rommel, the German army officer in charge. He later made excellent use of his 8.8cm FlaK guns in North Africa against Allied tanks. A typical German army tactic involved luring enemy tanks into the killing zone of the camouflaged 8.8cm FlaK guns. German gun crews would then use the superior range of their guns to destroy their opponents before the tanks could defend themselves with their shorter-range weapons.

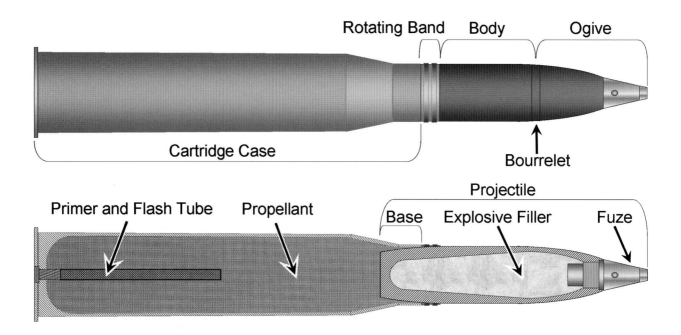

This drawing shows the various external parts of a generic high-explosive (HE) fixed round. Fixed means the projectile is crimped to the metal cartridge case that contains the primer and propellant. The primer ignites the propellant in the cartridge case, which burns fast and produces rapidly expanding gas that propels the projectile out a gun barrel. *James D. Brown*

VEHICLE-MOUNTED 8.8CM GUNS

The success of 8.8cm FlaK guns as antitank weapons in Spain, France, Russia, and North Africa led to the German army mounting them on a variety of self-propelled (SP) mounts. By simply placing the 8.8cm guns on a turret-less tank hull, the Germans could field a weapon system that could effectively repel enemy tank fleets until the Panther medium tank and the Tiger heavy tanks could take their place.

The distinction between a World War II tank and self-propelled (SP) gun derives from the way the main gun was mounted. The German military defined a tank as a fully tracked armored vehicle fitted with a gun in a crew-operated, 360-degree, traversable turret. In contrast, German SP guns of World War II had a fixed armored superstructure, which constrained the main gun to a very limited arc of fire.

The requirements for a gun on an SP mount were somewhat different from the standard 8.8cm, L/56 FlaK guns, so a redesign came about to optimize the gun for this application. To minimize recoil, the designers enclosed the barrel in a light jacket and added a muzzle brake. Originally, this gun was to go onto three

prototype vehicles (on a Panzer IV chassis). However, development of a longer and superior L/71 version of the 8.8cm gun with SP mount compatibility came along, so the 8.8cm, L/56 SP project ended.

During this same period, a Krupp-designed and -built turret appeared with an 8.8cm, L/56 gun (similar to that of the recently canceled 8.8cm, L/56 SP) mounted on what would become the first version of the famous Tiger tanks. The 8.8cm, L/56 gun designed for mounting in a tank turret was equipped with vertical sliding breechblocks, contrasting with the horizontal breech-blocks of all the various 8.8cm FlaK guns. The official designation of the new tank gun was the *KwK 36*. *KwK* is a German abbreviation for *Kampfwagen Kanone* ("combat vehicle gun").

AMMUNITION DIFFERENCES

A round of ammunition comprises all of the components necessary to fire a weapon once. Most World War II tank main gun rounds included a primer and propellant contained within a metal cartridge case, with the cartridge case crimped to the rear of a projectile so that it could be loaded into the breech of a tank gun in a

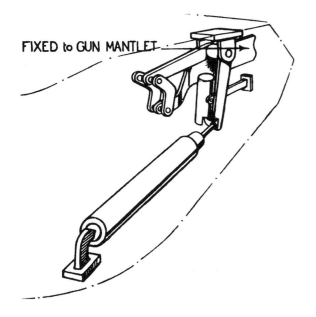

FIXED to GUN MANTLET

The early– and mid-production Tiger E tanks featured a spring equilibrator located on the loader's side of the tank, just above the turret ring, as seen here in this British army illustration. It aided in keeping the muzzle-heavy 8.8cm main gun balanced in the tank's turret. The spring equilibrator in the Tiger E tank attached to the gun shield.

single motion. The primer ignited the propellant and produced a great deal of hot, high-pressure gas that forced the projectile out the muzzle end of the bore.

FlaK versions of the 8.8cm gun used percussion-primed ammunition whose primers were detonated by a blow from a firing pin. In contrast, all main gun ammunition fired from the 8.8cm gun of both versions of the Tiger tank was electrically primed. When the Tiger gunner pulls the trigger, an electrical switch closes and passes current to a resistance wire that generates heat in the primer compound, causing the primer to detonate. The primer detonation in turn sets off the propellant in the cartridge case. Allied tank main guns still used a percussion-primed firing system throughout the war.

Electrically primed ammunition is slightly safer than percussion primed ammunition because it is less sensitive to being inadvertently struck as the ammunition is being handled in a tank. Although electrically operated primers may seem a little more sensitive to the stray electric spark, in fact, static electricity will not set them off. They require an electrical current to pass from a central contact point to a grounded cartridge case to set them off.

Beginning in July 1943, new production Tiger E tanks had the spring equilibrator moved to a vertical position at the rear of the turret, just to the right of the vehicle commander's seat, as seen here in this picture. The spring equilibrator attached to the rear of the 8.8cm main gun recoil guard with a roller chain. *Frank Schulz*

Electrically primed firing systems are simpler, because the gunner's trigger pull need only complete an electrical circuit and does not need a mechanical connection to strike the primer. Electrical safeties can be placed anywhere in the firing circuit. Mechanical firing pins are subjected to high shock levels during firing of the main gun, so they are subject to breakage and misalignment.

TIGER TANK GUN COMPONENTS

The 8.8cm gun barrels in both versions of the Tiger tank turrets mounted onto cylindrical steel trunnions recessed into either side of the front of their turrets. The trunnions allowed the gun barrels to be elevated or depressed and supported the weight of the gun barrels and their gun mounts.

Trunnions are normally placed were a gun barrel is roughly in balance. A slight degree of muzzle heaviness

continued on page 62

BERENT ISENBERG
TIGER TANK BATTALION 504, AUGUST 1944 TO FEBRUARY 1945

In the summer of 1941, at the age of sixteen, I entered into a pre-military training program that all young men of my age had to attend in Germany. During this training program, I received instructions on the use of small arms and some close combat fighting techniques. The following year, after finishing school in June, I had to perform three months of work service for the government before entering the army.

During the three-month work service period, my schoolmates and I received spades instead of rifles. Despite using the spades for our work duties, we had to keep them spotless and shiny at all times. Our assignment was to level the ground at a German air force fighter base. We did this by hand with the help of wheeled carts on tracks that we pushed around by hand.

In the fall of 1942, I entered into the army as a volunteer for tank service. I believed that I was a good candidate for tanks, because I had demonstrated a keen mechanical aptitude with my family's farm tractors. The army sent me to the town of Bielefeld in Westphalia, Germany, as part of Panzer Group 11. They were then using the Panzer III and IV tanks. Because I had already received pre-military training, my basic training period turned out to be very short.

Before we learned how to drive and operate the tanks, they made us take driver-training courses on passenger cars and then on trucks. The truck-driving part of our schooling involved hauling supplies to our base, while the rest of the time we spent loading and unloading the cargo on our trucks.

Only after we successfully completed the car- and truck-driving courses did we begin training on the Panzer III and IV tanks. It began with training on stationary vehicles, so that we knew every square inch of our tanks. Much of this stationary-vehicle training took place inside large buildings made completely dark to increase our familiarity with the tanks.

During our driver training time on the Panzer III and IV, they took small groups of us out on turretless versions of the tank. Each one of us got a chance to drive the tank with a sergeant instructor sitting just behind and on top of the open driver's hatch. I remember on one occasion that I did something that displeased the instructor while driving a tank, and he hit me over the head with a metal traffic sign he used to indicate right or left turns.

After our training program on the Panzer III and IV tanks was finished, a small number of us went into another training unit intended for reserve officer candidates. We received two short silver bars that identified us as such. The training for this course proved physically rigorous and demanding in the classroom. A lot of the classroom time involved playing war games in a great big sandbox that was about the size of two pool tables.

The sandbox had contours made with the sand and little trees. There were also little wooden models of tanks, half of them red and the other half blue. With these toy tanks, we learned the best way to approach the enemy and take advantage of the terrain while doing so. One important thing they taught us in the classroom for all drivers is when you came to a point were the enemy was visible, you should always pull the tank a little bit to the right or left, so that the front of the vehicle was not straight on against the enemy, but at an angle, so that any hits from the enemy would deflect off the tank's armor.

During the very difficult reserve officer training course, some of my fellow students failed, but I completed it successfully and then found myself promoted to private first class by the end of 1943. In January 1944, a dozen or so officer candidates, including myself, went off to the town of Paderborn, the training base for Panther and Tiger I tanks. Before this time, I did not know that either tank existed.

Berent Isenberg, in his black tanker's uniform, poses for a picture by his mother while visiting his family farm during a brief leave.

Our six-month training on the Tiger tanks at Paderborn proved extremely detailed. We were all cross-trained in the five crew positions on the tank: tank commander, gunner, loader, radioman, and driver. Our primary training as future officers focused on us being gunners with some overlapping training as tank commanders. I also remember during the training on the tanks that the instructors constantly reminded all of us that the Tiger was an expensive vehicle and the army could not afford to lose any because of human error.

Learning to drive the Tiger tank at Paderborn proved very different from driving the Panzer III and IV tanks with their manual transmission and simple clutch and brake steering. The Tiger had a complicated automatic transmission and a half steering wheel that you turned left or right, just like in a car. When the Tiger tank transmission was in neutral and you turned the steering wheel all the way to one side, it would make the inside track go backward and the outside track go forward. This allowed the tank to turn on a dime without pushing too much dirt around.

The driver on the Tiger tank had a small lever to his right, with eight forward speeds and three reverse gears. If you wanted to upshift, you needed to place the shift lever into the next notch and the shifting was done automatically. This worked very well in the mid-range. On the lower range, when you started out, you had to go from first to second. That was the hardest thing to shift, because the tank did not have the rolling capacity of a car. Before the shift could even be completed, the tank would almost stop again. On level ground or on a hard surface road, you could start out in second gear and then go right into third gear, without dealing with the very difficult first gear.

During gunnery practice with the 88, we fired on both stationary and moving targets. The latter were wooden mock-ups made to look like tanks. Steel cables and a winch that was perpendicular to our firing positions pulled the moving targets. This took place near Paderborn at the Senne, the tank proving grounds.

At the end of our training cycle on the Tiger tank, this being August 1944, we had the choice of three different assignments, all with Tiger tank units. The Western Front, the Eastern Front, which we knew was a very cold and nasty place, and sunny Italy. There were six of us at the time, and we all chose Italy and went off to Tiger Tank Battalion 504.

My first job with Tiger Tank Battalion 504 was to deliver food, ammunition, fuel, and engine oil during the night. We used a half-track for that job, which we called in German, the "coffin on wheels." My second job with the unit turned out to be as a loader. In a Tiger, every newcomer starts out as a loader, regardless of rank.

The one incident I remember vividly as a loader in a Tiger tank occurred when I inhaled too much gaseous fumes from the breech of the gun after firing and passed out. Luckily, I did not have my hands and arm in the way of the recoiling gun. This happened despite a vacuum system to purge the air inside the turret. When I passed out, the radioman crawled back from his position in the front of the tank's hull and took my place until I recovered a few minutes later. I was not hurt physically but suffered a great deal of embarrassment from that incident.

In September 1944, a gunner's position opened up in another tank, and I moved into that spot and remained there for the duration of my time in Italy, always with the same crew. That was from September 1944 to February 1945—about five months. With the move to the gunner's position, I received a promotion to sergeant.

During my time in Italy, with the 504 Tank Battalion, we were fighting a defensive war— not a typical job for tanks. We did a lot of sitting, looking, and waiting for our opposition to make a move. We were on duty around the clock, twenty-four hours a day, seven days a week. We generally took turns sleeping in a sitting position in our seats. On rare occasions, we had a layover farther behind the front lines in order to have a service or repair performed on our tank. It was then when we got several hours of sleep and maybe a place to wash our clothes.

When I look back on my Tiger tank service many years ago now, I'm still surprised by one thing, which is why we were not given periodic rest periods during our time on the front lines. We were informed in training repeatedly that human error must not occur, period! Yet, how can you do this by living in a tank twenty-four hours a day, seven days a week, with no washing, no shaving, and still keep your wits about you? I don't know. We were a sorry-looking bunch with body odor like over-ripe cheese. We were always tired and only when there was combat action did our adrenaline kick in and keep us going. For more routine work, we were like zombies.

I do remember one three-day rest period that we had when our transmission needed replacement. Two half-tracks, working in tandem, towed our tank to a repair base. To ease the towing process, the tank's two drive shafts, from the transmission to the reduction gears, were disconnected. When we arrived at the repair site, there was an A-frame set up to take the turret off of our tank. Then we rolled out the tank from under the turret. A second A-frame then aided in the removal of the damaged transmission and then helped to install the new one before the turret went back on the tank's hull.

Any repairs on the tank's tracks were our responsibility. Our most common problem with the track links were the steel pins that held them together. They often worked themselves free on the inside of the track, due to lateral pressure, and came out far enough to rub on the tank's hull with a terrible screeching noise. It was our job to pound the pins back in with a sledgehammer. This could be done only at the front of the vehicle where the tracks protruded out from the hull. To make the hammering of the pins go a little bit easier, we would reduce the tension of the track by turning a large nut with a socket wrench and a steel bar. At the end of this procedure, we restored the track tension.

While on duty along the front lines, our food came to us once daily, mainly at night when the supply trucks were not bothered by Allied planes. The meal was always a kind of stew or soup, with pieces of vegetables and meat floating in it. Then we would get some bread, butter, and sausage to take care of the other meals. We also scrounged for additional food from the local population. Along with the food, we received other needed supplies. These items had to be unloaded and stored before we could eat our "wonderful" meals.

The climate in northern Italy is very similar to California, with the days warm to almost hot and the nights cool to cold. We took our uniform jackets off during the day and put them back on at night. We did not have any overcoats or sweaters for the cooler parts of the day and had to depend on blankets to keep us warm. Because there was no laundry service, we had to wash our own uniforms and underwear whenever we had a chance. To relieve ourselves, we would climb out of the tank and go behind the vehicle. When there was shooting going on and we had to urinate, we used a tin can inside the tank.

We stayed one or two days in the same position and then moved at night to a new position selected for us by the higher ups. By daybreak, we had to have our camouflage material in place and the last several hundred yards of our track markings obliterated, fearing that Allied planes would spot our location by following the marks on the ground and determine our hidden positions. If we found a suitable house, we would back the Tiger into it with only the gun barrel sticking out. We then had to camouflage only the front of the vehicle. This type of position was much preferred on rainy days because our tank leaked like a sieve.

On my tank, we were very lucky to have a driver who had a lot of experience from serving in Russia on smaller tanks. The guy had a sixth sense, a nose for when something did not look right. Also, he could read the tank commander's brains and would often do something even before the commander could order it over the intercom.

My tank commander was a higher ranking, noncommissioned officer and, in civilian life, a baker. He was a very kind man, got a little excited when things were happening, but he was always very clear in his instructions. The loader was a nondescript small guy, very muscular and well trained for his job. The radioman was, in civilian life, a goldsmith. I don't know how a goldsmith, baker, and student found their way all into one tank.

To save battery power for the engines to start, we did not use the tank's radio except for designated times when we received orders for the next day. Infantry soldiers were always around us for protection, and we could talk back and forth with them.

The key moment for us to do something was just before sundown. During the day, we would have identified enemy positions that we would open fire upon with the setting sun. This gave the enemy no time to pinpoint our locations and open fire on us. We used armor-piecing rounds on the tanks and high-explosive rounds on trucks, buildings, and infantry soldiers. If an enemy tank faced me straight on, I fired at the turret ring. Even if the round didn't penetrate, it might dislodge or jam his turret. If the enemy tank sat at a 45 degree angle to me, I would aim for the lower rear portion, between the tracks, where their ammunition was stored.

When confronted with enemy tanks, it proved of crucial importance to deliver the first shot—and to make sure the first shot was a hit. This would cause some confusion on the enemy side, enabling us to get off a second shot before they had a chance to fire back on us. We are talking about a timeframe of about one minute. This was a highly successful tactic passed down to me by many seasoned tankers.

The high-explosive round we fired had a delayed-action fuse built into it. When we were firing at enemy infantry on flat ground, I aimed at the ground in front of them so that the round would bounce off the ground and then explode above their heads. If there was a large tree behind the enemy troops or, say, an antitank gun, I aimed at the tree trunk. The round would go off behind and over their heads, and the fragments would even reach into dugouts and foxholes.

The sight I used was an optic for one eye, but it had a piece where you would put your entire forehead. The optic enlarged the picture that you looked at—so that the tank or people that were one kilometer away appeared very clearly. In the optic, we had graduations built in, which allowed us to measure a tank's length. From that information, we could estimate the distance to the tank. The graduations in the optic were horizontal and vertical. The vertical part was the one used for longer distances when you had to elevate the gun a little more for super elevation.

We were normally between 1 kilometer and 1.6 kilometers from the enemy lines. This was well within our shooting range without having to make super elevation adjustments for either the armor-piercing or high-explosive rounds. The only occasion in which we engaged

Allied forces at longer ranges took place at an airport that we attacked. If I remember correctly, the distance upon which we engaged the enemy units was a little more than two kilometers. As this battle took place during the daytime, we had a great advantage with our longer-ranged gun.

In regard to the total number of kills my tank made in combat, I have always tried to avoid that question because it involves death and injury to Allied soldiers and tankers. I can answer that by saying that when I fired the Tiger's 88 at a target, there was always smoke, and on dry days, a lot of dust being kicked up. This tended to hide the actual strikes from my view. I depended on the tank commander to tell me if I had struck the target. As soon as the smoke from the firing cleared, the tank commander was pointing out the next target, or sometimes the same target again.

When several Tigers were firing, two of us could be shooting at the same target. We later hashed out who would get credit for which kills. The credits were never in writing—only verbal—and the credit goes to the tank commander who shares that glory with his crew. During my time as a gunner, my tank commander, received credit for seven tanks and numerous half-tracks, as well as two antitank guns. For my contribution, I received a decoration—a tank assault badge in silver.

The only hit on my tank came from what we thought was an antitank gun. The round struck the turret on the left front corner. The noise was a very loud bang on the inside as if somebody had struck the outside of the tank with a huge sledgehammer. The tank vibrated from this hit, which luckily for all did not penetrate.

In February 1945, my time as an officer candidate in the field was over, and I had to report to Germany for officer training school. I asked my commanding officer to change my order and keep me there because I was very happy being with the crew on my tank. I could also see the handwriting on the wall as to how the war was going, but my commanding officer said they needed officers and I had to go, which I did.

I arrived back in Paderborn, the tank training school, to find that it had been heavily bombed. There was no more officer training school, no running water, and no kitchen. There was nothing! I ended up in a unit that consisted of men from the army, navy, and air force. Everybody asked the question, "What the hell are we doing here?" Somebody gave us rifles, machine guns, and Panzerfausts, but there was no organization. We were lucky that the Allied forces quickly rounded us up as POWs. That was February 1945 and the end of my career as a Tiger tank man.

The two hooks hanging downward from the roof of a Tiger E tank turret over the breech end of the 8.8cm main gun make up the internal travel lock that held it in place and took inertia loads off the elevating gearbox when not in combat. Visible just above the breech end of the 8.8cm main gun is the loader's vision slit, protected by thick ballistic glass. *Andreas Kirchoff*

continued from page 55
is always desirable because it takes the backlash out of the elevation gears, but excessive weight bias toward the muzzle end of a gun barrel makes it hard to elevate. The Tiger E tank trunnions could not be placed at the 8.8cm gun's balance point. To compensate for the imbalance, the Germans installed a spring "equilibrator" in the vehicle so that the gun could be elevated without difficulty.

The spring equilibrator on the Tiger E tank originally appeared on the right side of the turret ring next to the loader's position and attached to the gun mount. Beginning with production units in July 1943, an improved spring equilibrator appeared at the rear of the Tiger E turret ring (just to the right of the tank commander's position). The new equilibrator attached to the main gun recoil guard with a roller chain.

Due to the well-chosen trunnion location on the Tiger B tank turret, there was no need to mount a spring equilibrator in the vehicle to balance the very long main gun barrel.

On the Tiger E tank, the trunnions actually extended out on either side of the turret, just behind the gun shield, and acted as lifting points for removing the turret from the tank with an overhead crane. A third lifting point was located at the rear centerline of the turret and normally hidden from view by the externally fitted rear turret storage box.

There were two types of 8.8cm barrels on the Tiger B tank, a single-piece (mono-bloc) barrel that appeared on some of the early Krupp/Porsche turrets and a sectional two-piece barrel, which began appearing on new production Tiger B tanks beginning in April 1944. Some new production Tiger B tanks appeared with the mono-bloc barrels as late as June 1944.

An internal elevation travel lock was just above the Tiger E main gun mount. The lock consisted of two connected hooks that hung from the roof of the turret and connected to studs on either side of the main gun breech. This excerpt from a Tiger E tank battalion report implies that there must have been problems with the travel lock: "The travel lock for the weapon must be capable of being operated with a handle. The ability to fire suffers due to the current travel lock and leads to delays of at least one minute. Under battle conditions, movement without locking down the weapon is not possible, as the weapon shows serious elevation alignment problems very quickly."

A modified internal travel lock that was easier to release began appearing on Tiger E tanks in April 1943. In November 1943, an external travel lock at the right rear of the hull appeared. This modification later disappeared and went on to be replaced by a further revision of the internal travel lock that now held the main gun at 15 degrees elevation when locked into place. The Tiger B tank also had an internal travel lock that held its main gun at 15 degrees elevation when locked into place.

The 8.8cm guns on the Tiger tanks had one of two types of double-baffle muzzle brakes. The smaller and lighter of the two appeared on both versions of the tank beginning in the summer of 1944.

A muzzle brake is a cylindrical extension for a cannon muzzle that redirects and partially dissipates the high-pressure gasses that follow the projectile out of the barrel. When redirected, a muzzle brake reduces recoil energy by directing the gas flow to the sides rather than along the barrel. The muzzle brake also cuts down on the amount of dust and dirt thrown up by the muzzle blast of a large-caliber gun. This was a very important factor for World War II German tank crews because they lacked the ability to fire on the move with any degree of accuracy and needed to fire from a stationary position to see the fall of their shot. Depending on the fall of the shot, the Tiger tank crew then decided if another round was necessary and adjusted for additional shots.

U.S. Army major Philip C. Calhoun commented in a World War II report about the advantage that muzzle brakes provided to the German Panther and Tiger tanks:

> The 75 and 88 on the Mark V [Panther] and Mark VI [Tiger] are superior to the 90mm [mounted on the U.S. Army M36 tank destroyer], partly because of the higher velocity and flatter trajectory, thus making it more possible for them to hit what they point at and partly because of the muzzle brake, which we have seen on the Mark V and Mark VI, thus allowing them to observe their fire better than our 90mm gunners or destroyer commanders can.

Recoil is the backward movement of a gun tube after being fired. The backward movement is the reaction to the force that provides the forward motion to a projectile. Counter-recoil is the forward movement of a gun

Located above the gun housing and barrel of an 8.8cm main gun, inside the turret of a Tiger B tank, are the two long cylinders that comprise the tank's recoil system. A recoil system is a mechanism designed to absorb the energy of recoil gradually and so avoid violent movement of the gun mount. *Frank Schulz*

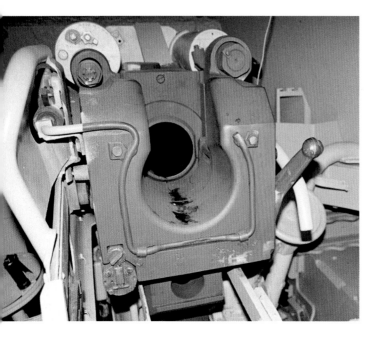

Visible is the breech housing of the 8.8cm main gun on a Tiger B tank. In this picture, the vertical sliding-wedge breechblock is in the open position. The piping around the edges of the breech housing is the manifold for the air that discharges down the gun barrel to clear propellant gasses. *Michael Green*

tube and connecting parts returning to their original position after recoil. The recoil system found on all large-caliber tank guns is a mechanism designed for gradually absorbing the energy of recoil to lower the forces on the mounting structure and prevent violent movement of the vehicle.

The recoil gear of the Tiger tanks was the typical German hydro-pneumatic recuperator on the left and a pneumatically operated counter-recoil buffer (shock absorber) on the right. A recuperator is that part of a tank's recoil mechanism that stores energy needed to return the barrel to its original firing position. When a Tiger's 8.8cm gun fired, the recoil would push the gun breech rearward almost two feet. Hydro-pneumatic is a combination of oil and air components that together behave like a spring and damper.

The breech of the Tiger tank's 8.8cm guns featured a semi-automatic vertical-falling breechblock, with an electrical safety device that prevented the firing of the weapon if the breechblock was open, the gun was not back in its original firing position, or the hydraulic buffer was not full. A breechblock is the principal

moving part of a gun's breech housing, which opens for loading a main gun round and closes for firing. It consists of a large, heavy steel block at the rear of a barrel that seals the rear end of the gun tube so that all of the propelling force goes toward the muzzle.

Upon firing, the metal cartridge cases expand against the walls of the chamber, sealing it and preventing hot, high-pressure powder gases from venting into the turret. As a tank's main gun counter-recoils, extractors located in the breech catch the rear lip of the now spent metal cartridge case and pull it from the chamber, making it ready for the loader to quickly insert a new round into the breech.

Berent Isenberg, a Tiger E tank crewmember, recalls that their supply trucks always retrieved their spent 8.8cm main gun cartridge cases for reuse. The problem was that the factories doing the reloading of the main gun rounds did not resize the spent cartridge cases properly. This surfaced when some newly delivered main gun rounds became jammed in the breech of their tank's cannon. After this occurred the first time, the tank's loader checked all the main gun rounds before using them in combat.

When a Tiger tank loader inserted an 8.8cm round into the chamber, he pushed it in far enough for the front end of the projectile to nestle in the forcing cone. The forcing cone is the forward end of a gun's chamber that tapers down to the bore, which has a constant diameter to the front or muzzle end of the gun. The forcing cone is where the soft metal rotating band (also known as the driving band) on the rear of the projectile engages the rifling in the gun's bore. The rotating band transmits rifling torque to the projectile. An obturator, which prevents propellant gases from escaping past the projectile, may be a separate feature or may be combined as a single piece with the rotating band.

TIGER E TANK MAIN GUN ROUNDS

Because German tactical doctrine made wide use of the 8.8cm guns as antitank weapons, a number of specially designed antitank rounds came into use for the weapon. The most widely employed antitank round on the Tiger E tank, the *Panzergranate* 39 (Pzgr 39), was thirty-four inches long and weighed thirty-three pounds. The full-bore projectile portion of the round was twelve inches in length. In British military terminology, it was an armor-piercing cap with a streamlined ballistic cap (APCBC) round. In World War II American military terminology, it was an armor-piercing capped (APC) round.

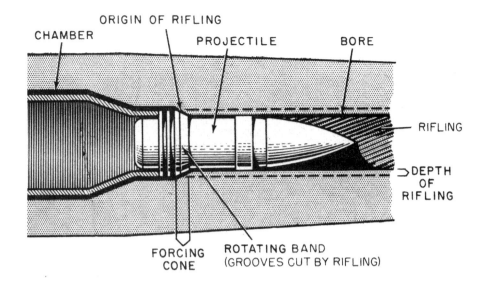

This U.S. Army illustration shows a cross-section of a gun chamber with a fixed round inserted into a rifled barrel. Highlighted in the drawing is the chamber where the cartridge case sits and the forcing cone where the rifling grooves engage the rotating bands of a projectile. The cartridge case does not engage with the rifling.

The twenty-two-pound, solid-hardened-steel, full-bore projectile of the Pzgr 39 contained a small HE bursting charge. The bursting charge detonated after the projectile penetrated the armor of a tank. The British military referred to the Pzgr 39 with the HE charge as an APCBC-HE round.

The full-bore Pzgr 39 projectile traveled at about 2,650 feet per second and could penetrate more than four inches of steel armor sloped at 30 degrees at a range of five hundred yards. This round could penetrate three inches of 30 degree–sloped armor at a range of one mile. Steel armor sloped at 30 degrees was the German army standard for qualifying the theoretical penetration abilities of its tank-killing projectiles.

A translated April 27, 1943, German military document from a book entitled, *Panzer Truppen 2: The Complete Guide to the Creating and Combat Employment of Germany's Tank Force, 1943–1945*, edited by Thomas L. Jentz, discusses the effectiveness of the Pzgr 39 rounds against T34 Russian tanks:

> First round hits were usually achieved with the 8.8cm KwK gun at ranges of between 600 to 1,000 meters. At these ranges, the *Panzergranate* absolutely penetrated through the frontal armor of T34 tanks. After penetrating through the frontal armor, usually the *Panzergranate* still destroyed the engine at the rear of the tank. In very few cases could the T34 be set on fire when fired at from the front. Shots from the same range hitting the side of the hull toward the rear or the rear of the tank resulted in 80 percent of the cases in which the fuel tanks exploded. Even at ranges of 1,500 meters and longer, during favorable weather, it is possible to penetrate the T34 with minimal expenditure of ammunition.

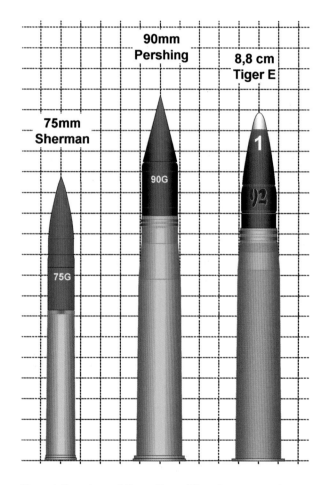

The relative sizes of these three AP main gun rounds provide an estimate of their comparative power. At left is the 75mm of the American M4 Sherman; at center is the 90mm of the American M26 Pershing heavy tank. The Pershing's gun, although not available until late in the war, finally provided a match for the firepower of the Tiger E tank, whose AP cartridge appears at the right.
James D. Brown

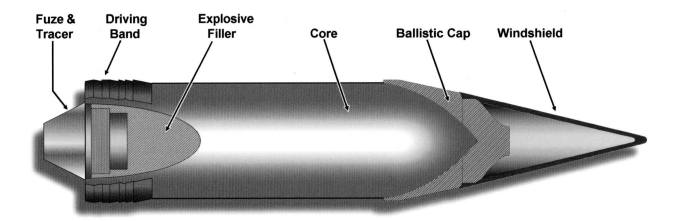

Fuze & Tracer **Driving Band** **Explosive Filler** **Core** **Ballistic Cap** **Windshield**

The ballistic windshield seen in this diagram of a generic APCBC projectile is a streamlined attachment designed to minimize air resistance to the projectile in flight. The job of the heat-hardened cap behind the windshield is to break the hardened outer crust of a tank's armor plate, causing it to weaken in order to make it easier for the core/body of the projectile to achieve penetration. *James D. Brown*

The crew members of a Tiger E tank are replenishing their vehicle with main gun ammunition. Visible in this picture is the loader's rear armored hatch and the large metal storage bin that attached to the rear of the tank's turret. Although the rear armored hatch opened from the inside, it had no spring mechanism to return it to its closed position, so somebody had to close it from the outside of the vehicle. *Patton Museum*

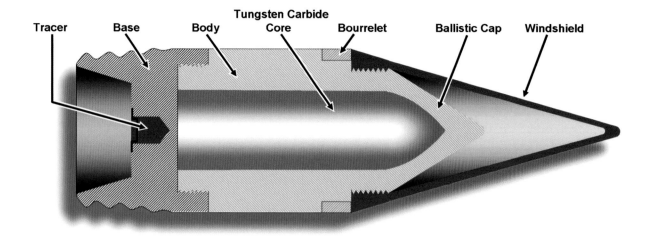

Tracer   Base   Body   **Tungsten Carbide**   Bourrelet   Ballistic Cap   Windshield
                                     Core

This diagram illustrates components of a generic HVAP projectile, whose construction is similar to the Pzgr 40 and Pzgr 40/43 fired from the 8.8cm main guns on the Tiger E and Tiger B tanks. Like a standard AP projectile, it has a ballistic windshield to cut down wind resistance in flight. *James D. Brown*

To fill certain main gun ammunition storage bins on the Tiger E tank, the crew had to rotate their turret to a rearward position, as is visible in this picture. This is not something normally done in the heat of combat, but it will often take place during lulls in action. Although a dangerous practice, crews on all sides often carried extra ammunition in extemporized stowage locations around the fighting compartment to avoid running out. *Patton Museum*

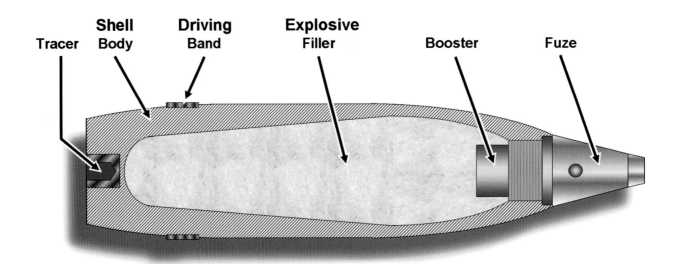

Tracer **Shell Body** **Driving Band** **Explosive Filler** **Booster** **Fuze**

Visible are the different components of a generic HE projectile. The fuse initiates the explosive element in a projectile at the time and under the circumstances desired. It also prevents initiation at other times. The primary target effects of such projectiles are blast, fragmentation, and concussion. *James D. Brown*

Another main gun round fired by the 8.8cm main gun on the Tiger E tank was the Pzgr 40 projectile. It traveled at three thousand feet per second. The British military nomenclature for this round was armor-piercing composite rigid (APCR) projectile. Unlike the Pzgr 39, it had no HE filler. In the American military, the Pzgr 40 would fall under the classification as a hyper-velocity armor-piercing (HVAP) round. It contained a sixteen-pound superhard tungsten carbide subcaliber core encased within a larger full-bore light alloy body. The body remained on the round all the way to the target before stripping off on impact. The theory of subcaliber APCR projectiles is that the energy of the core makes a smaller but deeper penetration in the target.

Although the 8.8cm gun on the Tiger E tank imparted less initial energy to the tungsten subcaliber core (520 kilojoules for Pzgr 39 and 422 kilojoules for Pzgr 40), the subcaliber core's armor penetration was superior to the full-bore Pzgr 39 projectile because of its smaller diameter. At a range of five hundred yards, the subcaliber Pzgr 40 projectile could penetrate six inches of steel armor. This was almost two inches more than the full-bore Pzgr 39 projectile at the same range. When the range went up to a bit more than a mile, the Pzgr 40 subcaliber projectile could still penetrate an

inch more of sloped steel armor than the full-bore Pzgr 39 projectile.

Due to a German wartime tungsten shortage, the Pzgr 40 was available only in very small numbers. A manual for the Tiger E tank recommended its use only when the Pzgr 39 could not do the job.

Both the Pzgr 39 and Pzgr 40 projectiles fired from the Tiger E tank 8.8cm gun are kinetic energy (KE) rounds. The kinetic energy of a projectile is the product of one-half the mass times the square of the velocity of the projectile in flight. To penetrate a target, KE projectiles rely on velocity and not an explosive charge. The HE bursting charge within the Pzgr 39 projectile was there to increase the amount of damage within the tank after penetration. The downside of HE bursting charges in KE projectiles is the cavities within the projectiles that contain the HE element often weaken the projectile's body and sometimes result in the projectile shattering on impact with the target.

Historical research indicates that KE projectiles are responsible for forty percent of tanks knocked out in battle. Because KE projectiles are normally fired at very high velocity, they have a very flat trajectory (flight path), a decreased time of flight, and increased hit probability. The effectiveness of KE projectiles decreases at longer ranges, since the projectiles slow down during long flights.

On the left of this picture is an 8.8cm Pzgr 39 AP round fired from the 8.8cm main gun on the Tiger E tank. On the right is a Sprengranate (Sprgr) HE fragmentation round for the same gun, intended for engaging thinly armored or nonarmored targets. Unlike the Pzgr 39 AP projectile, the HE projectile has an adjustable fuse on its tip. *Michael Green*

Full-bore HE rounds were also part of the Tiger E tank main gun inventory. In German, it was the *Sprengranate* (Sprgr). In its simplest form, an HE projectile consists of a hollow steel body containing an explosive charge with an impact fuse on the nose of the projectile. A post–World War II British army manual explains the characteristics of an effective HE round:

Caliber [size] is the principle factor affecting the lethality of the HE shell. In general terms, the larger the caliber, the greater the quantity of explosive filling. This in turn increases the lethal zone. However, muzzle velocity will also affect lethality since the higher the muzzle velocity required the thicker must be the walls of the shell body. This in turn reduces the amount of explosive filling and causes less effective fragmentation. Thus the most effective HE round should have a large caliber and a low muzzle velocity.

The Tiger E tank manual describes the main gun HE round:

The HE round is a high explosive shell, without a delayed action fuse, that produces shrapnel 20 meters to each side and 10 meters in the forward direction. It is effective against antitank guns, artillery, massed targets, and machine gun nests. It perforates gun shields, rips apart tires, tracks, loopholes, tips over vehicles, and sets everything on fire. Fitted with a delayed action fuse, it functions as a weapon against vertical targets, slamming through and exploding bunkers, houses, foxholes, forest, and early model enemy tanks. It will ricochet off of flat surfaces and then fly another 50 meters before exploding four to eight meters above locations which cannot be seen and could otherwise not be fired on.

TIGER E TANK SHAPED CHARGED ROUND

The Germans also developed a less-than-successful full-bore, shaped charged, high-explosive antitank (HEAT) round, known as *Hohlgranate, Hohlraumgranate,* or *Hohlraummunition* for the Tiger E tank's 8.8cm main gun, designated the Gr 38 HL or the HL/B-Granate. The seventeen-pound full-bore projectile traveled to a target at 1,950 feet per second.

Shaped charged projectiles differ significantly from AP projectiles in their principle of operation. Rather

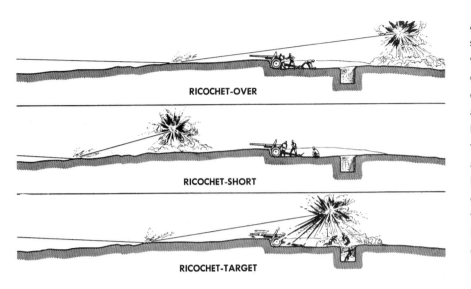

RICOCHET-OVER

RICOCHET-SHORT

RICOCHET-TARGET

An U.S. Army manual illustration shows how ricochet fire functions when engaging targets not easily engaged with direct fire. By employing an HE projectile with a delayed-action fuse and bouncing it off the ground in front of an enemy position, an airburst can be created that will kill troops without overhead cover. Although simple in theory, this technique requires as much luck as skill and is attempted only when mortar or artillery fire is not available.

The crew of a Tiger E tank is taking the time to clean the bore of their 8.8cm main gun with a brush mounted on the end of a long wooden pole. Cleaning the bore and chamber of a tank gun is required every time the weapon fires. This task is the key to prevent any corrosion of the bore or chamber due to the caustic elements contained within the propellant that would foul the weapon. *Patton Museum*

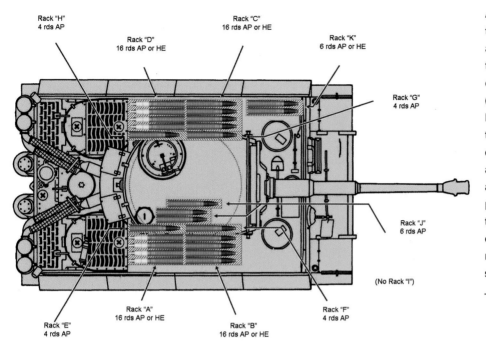

Rack "H"
4 rds AP

Rack "D"
16 rds AP or HE

Rack "C"
16 rds AP or HE

Rack "K"
6 rds AP or HE

Rack "G"
4 rds AP

Rack "J"
6 rds AP

(No Rack "I")

Rack "E"
4 rds AP

Rack "A"
16 rds AP or HE

Rack "B"
16 rds AP or HE

Rack "F"
4 rds AP

All racks on the right side of the Tiger E tank were accessible to the loader when the turret was to the front, but only the six rounds in Rack J (located under the turret basket floor) rotated with the turret. At other times, crewmembers passed ammunition from the less-accessible racks to the preferred storage locations in the right hull sponson. To complicate matters, not all racks could accommodate the slightly longer HE cartridges. *James D. Brown*

than using brute force to penetrate the armor plate on a tank, they focus an explosion at the point of impact. A shaped charged projectile's ability to penetrate armor is independent of its striking velocity. In fact, the shaped charge projectile itself remains at the outer face of the target tank's armor for a few microseconds (millionths of a second), which is required to focus the explosion and form the jet that produces the actual penetration. Passage of the jet through the target may erode destructive spall fragments as it penetrates through the armor. In addition to spall fragments, tiny, hot, high-velocity fragments of liner material from the projectile enter the tank, much to the detriment of the crew inside.

Early shaped charged projectiles lost a great deal of their ability to penetrate armor when fired from rifled guns because centrifugal forces acted against the explosive forces trying to collapse the liner to form the jet. Spinning the projectile also took energy that could be more effectively used for higher muzzle velocity. Shaped charged projectiles worked best during World War II when attached to fin-stabilized rockets fired from smoothbore barrels like the handheld American bazooka or its larger German counterpart, the *Panzerschreck* ("tank terror").

MAIN GUN AMMUNITION STORAGE

The Tiger E tank had storage space for ninety-two main gun rounds. No main gun rounds were stored in the

tank's turret. Sixty-four of the main gun rounds accessible to the loader lay horizontally in bins on racks (called panniers by the British), with thirty-two on each side of the upper hull. A British army report describes their arrangement:

These bins [four] are situated in the panniers on each side of the hull. The door of each bin is closed at the top by two toggle clips and is hinged at the center and bottom. When open, the doors fold down on the floor and do not foul the turret when it is being traversed. Each bin holds 16 rounds of AP or HE ammunition, stowed in four layers of four rounds each. The layers are each supported by three fixed horizontal steel arms connected by traverse strips. Each arm is shaped to fit the underside of the rounds. The first round of each layer is prevented from rolling by two spring retainer bars fitted to the two arms supporting the case of the round. The remaining three rounds in each layer are held in position by similar retainer bars, which are linked together and all three of which unlock as a single unit.

Another sixteen Tiger E main gun rounds were stowed horizontally on the hull floor, even with the bottom of the turret basket floor. Six more main gun

A Tiger E tank with its left-hand side turret and superstructure hull plates removed. Shows the space in the left-side superstructure in which thirty-eight of the 8.8cm main gun rounds were stored. Missing from this vehicle are the horizontal wooden and metal racks that would hold the rounds in place when loaded into this space. *Andreas Kirchoff*

rounds were stowed horizontally under the turret basket floor, while another six rounds were stored horizontally in racks alongside the driver's position.

An evaluation of the Tiger E main gun ammunition storage arrangement appears in a British wartime report:

> No immediate supply [main gun rounds] is carried on the turntable [turret basket floor] but the floor and pannier bins are very accessible for most turret positions. The method securing the rounds in the floor bins is simple, quick and accessible . . .
>
> The pannier bins, too, work quite well but the outermost rounds require a knack for quick removal. In fact, rapid withdrawal of ammunition necessitates learning the optimum procedure for each batch of rounds. This comes quickly with experience.

Despite the official main gun ammunition storage arrangements for all tanks, tankers of all nations in World War II tended to load up their vehicles with extra main gun rounds for fear of running out in battle. This was no doubt true with Tiger E tank crews as is reflected in an American intelligence publication dated April 1944, in which this quote appears from a captured Tiger tank crewmember: "A prisoner stated that his PzKw 6 [Tiger E tank] carried over 100 shells for the gun, 'stowed everywhere,' however, the standard ammunition load is 92 shells."

A British army report published in August 1944 quotes a Tiger E tank crewmember captured in Italy regarding main gun ammunition storage in his unit's tanks:

> PW [prisoner of war] stated that the normal stowage in a Tiger is 92 rounds but that the battalion has been increasing stowage in Italy to 106 rounds and even on rare occasions to 120 rounds by the addition of brackets for seven rounds each above the chambers already provided. It is not known whether this modification had been suggested within the battalion or whether it was carried out on instructions from Germany. The maximum stowage carried out by PW was 60 each of AP and HE rounds.

The German army officially sanctioned the extra main ammunition storage arrangement described in the previous quote in October 1944.

Berent Isenberg recalls that no Tiger E tank in his unit ever carried more than the authorized ninety-two main gun rounds during his time in Italy, and he typically fired only a few main gun rounds a day. He never had to access any main gun rounds in his tank other than those stored on his side of the vehicle in the right hull upper bins.

A captured German army report from 1943 on the Tiger E tanks employed in North Africa describes the division between types of main gun ammunition stored in the vehicles:

From the driver's position on a Tiger E tank, the forward right-hand-side superstructure main gun round bin (Rack B) is clearly visible. The sixteen-round bin located behind it (Rack A) is blocked from view by the turret basket. Also visible in this picture are the two small, closed main gun round boxes composing Rack F (each holding two rounds) located just below and in front of the two sixteen-round bins. *Frank Schulz*

This picture shows the six-round ammunition bin (Rack K) located to the left of the driver's position on a Tiger E tank. The sheet metal door that normally covered the main gun rounds from dust and dirt is in the folded position in front of the bin. All the main gun ammunition round bins in the Tiger E tank had sheet metal doors intended to keep the rounds from getting dirty. *Frank Schulz*

According to a captured document, the types of proportions of ammunition in use in the North African campaign were HE (25 percent) AP 38 APCBC (66 percent) and AP 40 (nine percent) . . .

These proportions give 23 rounds of HE, 61 rounds of APCBC and eight rounds of AP 40 per tank.

A British army report on the Tiger E tank dating from August 1944 describes the division between main gun rounds as found in a captured German army notebook as forty-two rounds of Pzgr 39, four rounds of Pzgr 40, and forty-six rounds of Sprgr.

WORK CONTINUES ON IMPROVING THE 8.8CM GUN

Although the original 8.8cm FlaK guns were effective against the aircraft in service before 1938, they became less and less effective as aircraft performance improved.

Although they were still deadly against the lumbering bomber fleets conducting the Allied strategic bombing campaign, none of the existing 8.8cm FlaK guns, nor the larger and heavier 12.8cm FlaK guns, proved capable of effectively dealing with faster and more agile Allied tactical aircraft.

Improving the existing 8.8cm FlaK guns proved to be more difficult than expected, so development contracts for a new 8.8cm FlaK gun were issued to both Krupp and Rheinmetall in May 1942. The German antiaircraft gun improvement program was closely related to the parallel designs for the new 8.8cm tank and antitank guns, which at that time were still designated the KwK 42, L/71 and the Pak 42, L/71. Pak was a German abbreviation for *Panzerabwehrkanone* ("antitank gun"). The Germans changed designations in

Because of the construction complexity of the towed four-wheel gun carriage on the 8.8cm, Pak 43 antitank gun, the Germans modified the two-wheel gun carriage of a medium artillery piece to accept the weapon, and with the addition of a new gun-shield, it became the 8.8cm Pak 43/41.
Michael Green

When Krupp's efforts to design and field a more powerful 8.8cm, L/71 antiaircraft gun failed to meet the German military's expectations, they devoted their efforts to seeing it fielded as a tank and a towed antitank gun. The tank gun version of the Krupp 8.8cm, L/71 ended up in the turret of the Tiger B tank. Pictured is the four-wheeled towed antitank version of that same gun, designated the 8.8cm Pak 43.
Michael Green

Due to the impressive penetrative powers of the AP projectiles fired from the Krupp 8.8cm Pak 43 gun, the Germans mounted it on a number of turretless tank destroyers. One of the most successful showed up on the chassis of the Panther medium tank and found itself referred to as the *Jagdpanther*. This particular example of a Jagdpanther resides in a Swiss army museum. *Andreas Kirchoff*

January 1943: the KwK 42, L/71 became the KwK 43, L/71 and the Pak 42, L/71 became the Pak 43, L/71.

As late as the winter of 1942, the new Krupp 8.8cm FlaK gun design was still favored by the German military over the competing Rheinmetall design because of Krupp's higher muzzle energy and trouble-free cartridge case extraction. Plans had called for the prototype's completion (designated the FlaK 42) by the spring of 1943 if no other alterations were required. However, various sources suggested lengthening the barrel to increase muzzle velocity. The extra work to create and test a new barrel and pressure of other design work resulted in the cancellation of the Krupp FlaK 42 gun program in February 1943.

THE ULTIMATE 8.8CM ANTITANK GUN

Despite work on the Krupp FlaK 42 gun program ending, the development of an antitank gun version

continued with the introduction of the Krupp-designed 8.8cm Pak 43, L/71. Various versions appeared on two different types of towed ground mounts and three different types of turretless tank destroyers: they included the *Jagdpanther* ("hunting panther"), the *Elefant* ("elephant"), and the *Nashorn* ("rhinoceros").

In parallel, the tank version of the Pak 43, designated 8.8cm KwK 43, L/71, was integrated into the new Tiger B heavy tank. The new gun used the same ammunition and was ballistically identical to the 8.8cm Pak 43, L/71 models.

The Krupp 8.8cm KwK. 43, L/71 was neither Hitler's first choice nor that of the weapon design office of the German army's Ordnance Department. Both preferred mounting a tank gun version of the 8.8cm FlaK 41, L/74 designed by Rheinmetall-Borsig for the Tiger B tank. However, the larger Rheinmetall gun and ammunition could not be easily integrated into either the Porsche or

An interim tank destroyer fitted with the Krupp 8.8cm Pak 43 gun was an open-topped vehicle based on a chassis composed of components from both the Panzer III and IV medium tanks. The Germans originally referred to it as the *Nashorn* ("rhinoceros") and later as the *Hornisse* ("hornet"). About five hundred units of this vehicle came off the production line between February 1943 and March 1945. *Michael Green*

Krupp turrets for the Tiger B tank, and the idea was dropped from consideration.

The 8.8cm KwK 43, L/71 gun showed a dramatic increase in performance over the earlier generation of 8.8cm guns on the fields of battle and went on to be considered the best anti-armor gun developed during World War II.

A translated November 25, 1944, German military document edited by Thomas L. Jentz discusses the effectiveness of the Tiger 8.8cm KwK 43, L/71 main gun during engagements with Soviet army tanks:

> In tank-versus-tank combat, the 8.8cm Kw.K. 43 gun is effective in destroying all of the types of enemy tanks, including the Stalin [IS-2 heavy tank armed with a 122mm gun], at ranges up to 1,500 meters. Under favorable conditions, the T34 [T34/76] and T43 [T34/85] tanks can also be knocked out at ranges up to 3,000 meters. As previously experienced in the West with Allied tanks, it was often observed that the Russian tanks declined to fight Tigers or

turned and fled after their first tank was knocked out. The same thing applies to the Russian assault guns as to the Stalin tanks. Kills at over 1,500 meters have not yet occurred.

A U.S. Army report dated September 13, 1944, describes details of the 8.8cm KwK 43, L/71 main gun on the Tiger B tank:

> An official German document states that the gun has an elevation of 15 degrees and a depression of eight degrees . . .
>
> The length of the ordnance from rear of the breech ring to end of barrel is 20 feet 8 inches. An air blast mechanism consisted of nozzles arranged [on] each side of the breech ring to direct jets of air into the chamber and prevent flame or gasses passing back into the turret while the breech is open.
>
> The standard full-bore AP round for the Tiger B tank's 8.8cm gun was an APCBC round known as the Pzgr 39/43, whose muzzle velocity of 3,340 feet per

The least successful version of a German tank destroyer armed with the Krupp 8.8cm Pak 43 gun was the Elefant ("elephant") based on the chassis of the failed Porsche candidate for the Tiger E tank competition. Rushed into service in the summer of 1943, without sufficient testing, the Elefant chassis proved unreliable in service and suffered serious mechanical problems. Most served in Russia and a few in Italy. *Michael Green*

second gave exceptional armor penetration performance. At a range of five hundred yards, it could penetrate more than seven inches of steel armor, six and a half inches at one thousand yards, and five inches at one mile.

The Pzgr 39/43 twelve-inch long, twenty-two-pound full-bore projectile was the same as the Tiger E tank projectile. However, to achieve the improved armor penetration results desired by the German military, the weapon's designers lengthened and enlarged the cartridge case diameter to hold more propellant. The full round was forty-four and a half inches long and weighed more than fifty pounds.

The main gun inventory of the Tiger B tank, like that of the Tiger E tank, comprised full-bore Pzgr 39/43 APCBC rounds and APCR rounds referred to as Pzgr 40/43. The sixteen-pound subcaliber projectile portion of the Pzgr 40/43 traveled to a target at 3,300 feet per second and could penetrate more than eight and a half inches of armor at five hundred yards. At one thousand yards, it could punch holes through

seven and a half inches of armor. At one mile, it could penetrate more than six inches of armor.

Like the Tiger E tank, the Tiger B tank's main gun also fired full-bore HEAT rounds designated Gr 39/43 HL. This round was capable of penetrating three and a half inches of armor at up to a range of one mile. HEAT projectiles can penetrate the same amount of armor regardless of range or the slope of the armor struck.

Charles Lemons, curator of the Patton Museum of Cavalry and Armor, which has a Tiger B tank on display, describes the procedure for loading and firing the 8.8cm main gun.

The loader brings the round from the turret rack [ready racks] or up front [from] the hull racks and inserts it into the gun. The breech closes and he steps off to the side, and pushes in the plunger on a safety box with his hand. That lights up a ready light for the gunner, who now knows the gun is ready to go. The

On display at the Patton Museum of Cavalry and Armor, located at Fort Knox, Kentucky, is this Tiger B tank, with the left side of its turret and hull superstructure cut away to reveal the interior of the vehicle. Visible in the pictures are the mannequins dressed in historical period uniforms at the tank commander and gunner's positions. *Michael Green*

gunner then lays the gun on target and fires. The gun immediately goes into recoil and the safety switch automatically switches the firing circuit off. As the gun returns to battery, the breechblock opens, ejecting the spent cartridge case. The gun then returns into full battery, ready for another round. Because of their size, I doubt if you would fire very many rounds before stopping to toss the empty cartridge cases out of the turret.

TIGER B TANK MAIN GUN AMMUNITION STORAGE

The number of main gun rounds stored in the Tiger B tank tended to vary. Tiger B production tanks with the forty-seven original Krupp/Porsche turrets appeared with horizontal storage space for only seventy-eight main gun rounds—sixty-two in the hull and sixteen in the rear turret bustle. The British and American armies referred to these as ready racks. The main gun storage plan for Tiger B tanks fitted with the Krupp/Henschel turret called for storage of eighty-six horizontally stored main gun rounds—sixty-four of them stored in the hull and twenty-two in the rear turret bustle ready racks. There seemed to be exceptions to the rule as the U.S. Army captured Tiger B tanks in late 1944 that had

storage racks for only forty-eight main gun rounds in the hull and the remaining twenty-two in the rear turret bustle ready racks. An October 16, 1944, report by 1st Lt. George B. Drury, attached to the First U.S. Army, documents this finding:

> A manual found in one of the tanks gives the designation of the tank as Tiger Model B. It is not known, however, whether this or Tiger II is the accepted nomenclature. Stowage space for 70 rounds of ammunition was found in the tanks. Sixty-nine rounds in one tank were accounted for and these consisted of 39 rounds of AP and 30 rounds of HE. Stowage of the ammunition was all in the sponson sides and turret rear.

To ease the Tiger B loader's job when accessing the main gun rounds in the turret ready racks, when the gun elevation was reasonably level, there was a collapsible roller, located in the rear of the turret in line with the 8.8cm gun's breech.

The collapsible roller might also have come in handy if somebody outside the tank decided to pass main gun rounds through the turret rear hatch for the loader who was standing inside the tank. As the main gun rounds came through the rear turret hatch, the loader could balance them on the roller for distribution to the hull and turret stowage racks.

A British army report on captured Tiger B tanks describes in detail the ready rack arrangement in the vehicles. It also described how the loader inserted the main gun rounds into the breech of the 8.8cm gun from the ready racks.

> The two "ready" racks in the vehicles are racks A and B, which are situated in the turret bulge. Rack A is in the right side of the bulge (nearer the loader) and rack B is on the left side. Each rack in the earlier vehicle [Krupp/Porsche turret] holds eight rounds, and in the more recent vehicle [Krupp/Henschel turret] 11 rounds. The rounds are stowed in three layers, each layer resting on two fixed arms. Each round is individually held in position by two steel straps fastened [with] toggle clips. Although this arrangement keeps the rounds securely in place, the rearmost clips are not easily accessible and time is lost both in fastening and un-fastening each round.
>
> The drill for loading from either rack is: remove the empty [cartridge] case from the gun and throw it through the [overhead] ejection hatch, move to the rack, undo the toggle clips holding the round, roll the round along the rack arms, lift (or drop) the round onto the roller, holding the ogive [nose cone] by the right hand, pull the round forward on the roller and guide the projectile into the breech (still holding the ogive by the right hand), push the base of the round with the left hand lifting it clear of the roller and deflector guard, and ram the round home. Operate the safety switch with the right hand.

In late 1944 and early 1945, Henschel came up with proposals to increase the main gun ammunition storage capability on the Tiger B tank. Nothing came of the proposals before the war in Europe ended.

TIGER TANK OPTICS

The effective use of any gun in the direct-fire mode depends on the weapon's crew being able to spot a target, engage it, and then destroy it in the shortest amount of time possible. One of the major contributing factors leading to the successful use of the 8.8cm gun as an anti-tank weapon during World War II was its outstanding optics (sights), which formed a key part of the gun's fire-control system. Because the German optics industry was

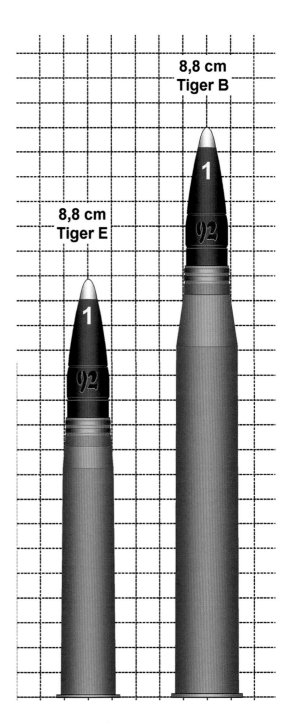

The Tiger B tank firepower was upgraded by lengthening the barrel from L/56 to L/71, with a concurrent increase in chamber volume to allow for more propellant. This illustration shows a size comparison of the 8.8cm main gun rounds fired from two different types of Tiger tanks. The Tiger E cartridge is on the left and that for the Tiger B is on the right. *James D. Brown*

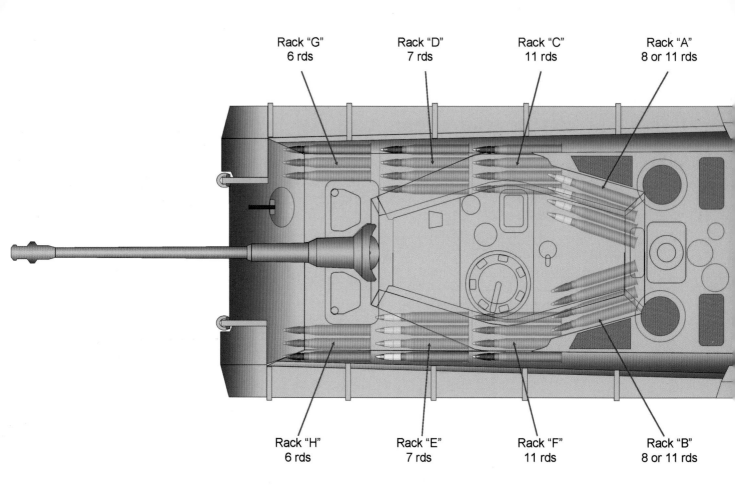

Rack "G"
6 rds

Rack "D"
7 rds

Rack "C"
11 rds

Rack "A"
8 or 11 rds

Rack "H"
6 rds

Rack "E"
7 rds

Rack "F"
11 rds

Rack "B"
8 or 11 rds

This illustration shows the location of the main gun rounds stored in a Tiger B tank with a Krupp/Henschel turret. There was a sheet metal shield between the rounds stored in the turret rear and the turret wall sides to protect them from spall generated when a projectile struck the exterior turret walls. Although Racks A and B rotated with the turret, only Rack A was accessible to the loader in all turret orientations. *James D. Brown*

the best in the world prior to World War II, German gunners could confidently engage opponents at ranges far in excess of their Allied counterparts.

According to German tank gunnery manuals, a Tiger gunner's odds for a first-shot hit on a tanklike target (whose range has already been determined) was 100 percent at five hundred yards. At one thousand yards, the odds of a first-shot hit were 93 percent for the Tiger E and 85 percent for the Tiger B tank. At a range of one mile, the first-shot hit odds dropped to 50 percent for the Tiger E and 43 percent for the Tiger B. At a mile and a half, the first-shot hit odds were 31 percent for both Tiger versions.

According to gunnery test results conducted by the British on captured Tiger E tanks, the accuracy of the KwK 36 8.8cm gun on the Tiger E tank was excellent. The test results appear following:

"A five round grouping of 16 x 18 [inches] was obtained at a range of 1,200 yards. Five rounds were fired

at targets moving at 15 mph and, although smoke obscured observation by the gunner, three hits were scored after directions were given by the commander. Normal rate of fire was estimated to be from five to eight rounds per minute."

While reticle marks in the sight allowed Tiger gunners to estimate the range to a target, the preferred process of estimating range was contained in a German manual:

"The distance can only be properly estimated by the driver and commander, because they can see the target unhindered with the naked eye. It is worse through the telescopic sight . . ."

Besides using their own eyes for estimating target range, Tiger tank commanders also employed binoculars, with a built-in range scale, to estimate target range. Then, by watching the trajectory and fall of the projectiles (equipped with tracer elements), the tank commander and driver could agree on a better gun position for the second shot. This went on until the target

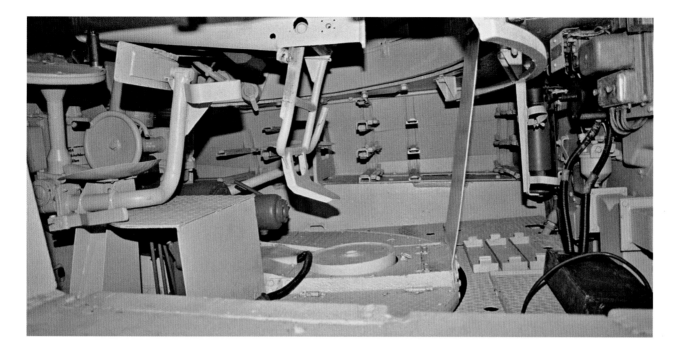

Looking into the cut-away left-side superstructure of a Tiger B tank, the gunner's seat and his manually operated traversing and elevation controls are visible, as are the various fixtures on the firewall between the crew's fighting compartment and the engine compartment. On the far side of the hull superstructure, the main gun ammunition racks are visible in this picture. *Michael Green*

sustained a hit or hits capable of rendering the target inoperable. The loader would continue to load the type of round first ordered by the tank commander unless he changed his mind.

A passage from a U.S. Army postwar gunnery manual describes the advantages and disadvantages of range estimation by eye.

> Estimation by eye is the most rapid but least accurate method of determining range. This method requires a great deal of training. Training must be continuous to maintain the proficiency necessary to estimate range by eye with any degree of accuracy. Accuracy is also greatly influenced by the distance to the target. As the range increases, accuracy decreases at a rapid rate.

Early and mid-production Tiger E tank commanders provided instructions over the intercom to the gunner using a clocklike turret position device graded from one o'clock to twelve o'clock. The arm for the twelve o'clock position always pointed forward. The second hand of the position device followed the position of the main gun. The tank commander had a matching counter-rotating turret posi-

tion indicator. The tank commander's azimuth indicator device disappeared from the Tiger E tank production run beginning in February 1944, as it did from the Tiger B tank.

Numerous factors can cause a tank main gun projectile to miss a target. These factors include the wrong initial range; the wrong lay, trunnion tilt, or wind; gun/gun sight misalignment; ammunition dispersion; faulty servicing of the sights; imprecise gun control or recoil equipment. Minor factors include air density, propellant temperature, and drift. Drift is a shift in projectile direction due to the cannon rifling and atmospheric conditions.

At ranges more than 1,300 yards (or when visibility was poor) Tiger E tank crews bracketed a target. Tiger B tank crews could usually engage targets without bracketing up to about two thousand yards, owing to the longer effective range of their version of the 8.8cm main gun.

Bracketing is a method of adjusting fire in which an imaginary bracket around an enemy target forms by firing over a target, then firing in front of the target along a spotting line, and then correcting the aiming point by splitting the imaginary bracket in half until the target sustains a hit.

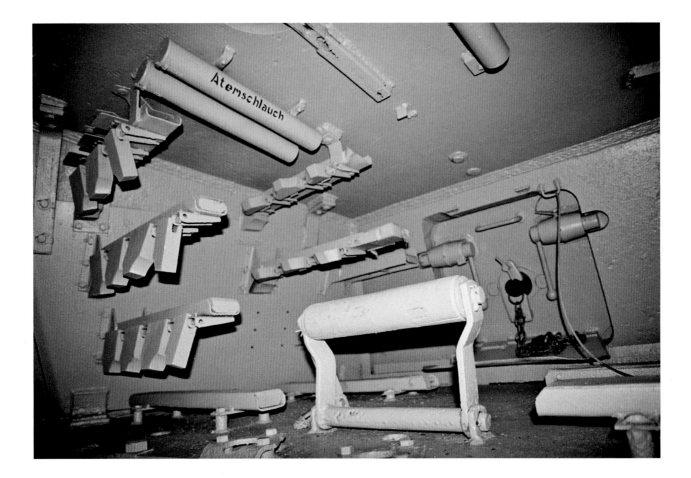

Looking backward and upward from the gunner's position on an Tiger B tank, some of the horizontal racks that held main gun rounds are visible in the turret bustle of the vehicle, as is the fold-down roller used by the vehicle's loader to assist him in manhandling the rounds into the breech of the 8.8cm main gun. *Michael Green*

Under near-perfect visibility conditions, Tiger E tank crews could successfully engage a stationary tank target at a mile and a half using bracketing. Tiger B tank crews were known to defeat stationary targets at more than two miles. At such extreme ranges, the Tiger tank gunners had to take into account super elevation. An explanation of *super elevation* appears in a postwar British army manual:

"A projectile fired from a gun at a point in line with the axis of the bore will not strike at that point, but will fall short owing to the effects of gravity on the projectile during its flight. To compensate for this it is necessary to elevate the gun so that it points above the object to be hit. This is the principle of giving elevation to a gun in order to hit the target."

The normal drop-off in first round accuracy of the Tiger tank main guns at ranges above a mile and a half

had to do with the lack of the sophisticated fire-control features found on modern tanks. Thermal imaging sights (to see in the dark and in poor weather conditions), laser range finders, cross-wind sensors, and full-solution solid state digital computers that instantly calculate all the ballistic variables almost guarantee a first round kill at ranges up to three miles even while moving. The Tiger tanks lacked any kind of stabilization system, so they could not fire with any accuracy while on the move.

With the advantage of a long-range main gun and a superior fire-control system for its day, both versions of the Tiger tank amassed an impressive kill ratio, according to author Christopher W. Wilbeck in his book titled *Sledgehammers: Strengths and Flaws of Tiger Tank Battalions in World War II*:

"Whatever mission heavy tank battalions were given, their primary task was to destroy enemy tanks. In

On the bottom of the turret basket floor of a Tiger B tank (painted in blue) is the vehicle's hydraulic turret traversing pump. Also visible is the gunner's elevation hand-wheel, with the firing handle located directly behind it and the gunner's is traversing hand-wheel. Behind the gunner's seat, under the diamond plate sheet metal box, is the vehicle's air compressor (also painted in blue). *Michael Green*

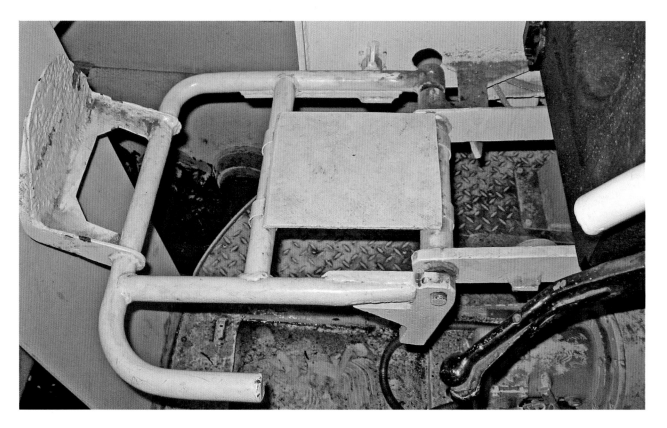

Instead of the canvas sack that caught the ejected spent main gun cartridge cases on the Tiger E tank, the Tiger B tank featured a foldable metal tray behind the breech housing. When a spent metal cartridge case ejected from the breech, it struck the deflector plate seen at the rear of the tray, and then dropped onto the tray, at which time the loader picked it up and hurled it out a small overhead hatch. *Frank Schulz*

Inside a Tiger E tank is the gunner's original articulated binocular sighting system fitted with a brow pad. The sighting system had a magnification of 2.5-power and provided the gunner with a 23-degree field of view. To the left of the sighting system is the gunner's vision slit, protected by thick ballistic glass.
Tank Museum, Bovington

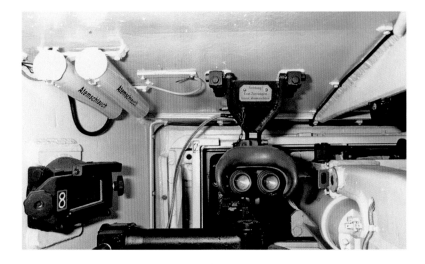

so doing, they were undeniably successful. The kill ratio of heavy tank battalions when measured against Tigers lost in direct combat is an impressive 12.2 to 1."

Interviews with Red Army tankers in *T34 in Action,* edited by Artem Drabkin and Olge Sheremet, point out the range advantage of the Tiger's 8.8cm main gun in comparison to the Soviet 76.2mm main gun on the T34/76 medium tank:

> Due to the fact that we only had 76mm guns, which could penetrate a Tiger's front armor from only a distance of 500 meters, the German tanks were deployed in the open. But just try to approach them, they'd burn your tank from 1,200 to 1,500 meters! They were cocky! In essence, until we got 85mm guns we had to run from Tigers like rabbits and look for an opportunity to turn back and get at their flanks. It was difficult. If you saw a Tiger 800 to 1,000 meters crossing you while it moved its gun horizontally you could stay in your tank. But once it starting moving vertically, you'd better jump out or you'd get burned. It never happened to me, but other guys bailed out.

TIGER FIRE-CONTROL SYSTEMS

Early tank designs had been fitted with straight-through telescope sights that attached directly to the main gun. While simple in design, this arrangement was awkward because the gunner had to follow the sight whenever the main gun moved up or down in elevation.

Gunners on early and mid-production Tiger E tanks had an articulated binocular (two-lens) telescopic sight known as the *Turmzielfernrohr* (TZF 9b) that featured an armored shutter. Articulated telescopic sights joined to a

tank's main gun have an eyepiece that remains in a fixed position for ease of the gunner's sighting. The TZF 9b sight had 2.5-power magnification.

Starting in March 1944, all production Tiger E tanks were fitted with articulated monocular (single-lens) telescopic sights designated TZF 9c. This optical sighting device gave the Tiger E Gunners a choice between two magnifications, either 2.5- or five-power. The five-power magnification came into use at longer ranges while the 2.5-power magnification, with its wider field of view, was for closer ranges.

The early Tiger B tank turrets were fitted with an articulated binocular TZF 9b/1 sight, with a magnification of 2.5-power. Beginning in April 1944, they began appearing with an articulated monocular telescopic sight designated the TZF 9d. Like the articulated TZF 9c telescopic sight in the Tiger E tank, it featured a choice between 2.5- or five-power magnification.

A British army report reviews the sighting system on the Tiger B tank with the articulated monocular telescopic sight designated the TZF 9d.

> The sight, type TZF 9d, is articulated at the front end, and the eyepiece is clamped to the turret roof. The sight is mounted about four inches to the right of the seat centerline and the gunner must lean to the right when sighting. The brow pad inspected was very hard, and the gunner would be liable to injure his nose on the eyepiece when sighting on the move. . . . No vision device other than the sight is provided for the gunner.
>
> In conclusion: The gunner's position is very unsatisfactory. It is cramped and uncomfortable and some of the controls are badly designed, and the gunner is given inadequate equipment.

All versions of the Tiger gunner's optical sight were limited to a narrow field view. This somewhat limited field of view is common for most tank gunners. Because of the superior overall view from the top of a tank, target acquisition and initial range-determination are normally the responsibilities of the tank commander, but assistance from other crewmembers was expected.

The Tiger gunner's monocular sight contained two illuminated transparent discs. The first disc had a range scale inscribed around the circumference. The gunner turned this disc until the appropriate range to a target was set against a small pointer. This action would simultaneously raise the other transparent disc, which incorporated the gunner's graticules (aiming marks). The gunner would then overlay the aiming marks on the target using his hand-operated elevation and traverse controls. By using the estimated width of a target, the gunner could make a rough range determination. This range-finding process is called the stadiametric range determining system.

While the stadiametric range determining system is a relatively quick, simple, and inexpensive method of finding the range to a target, it was not particularly accurate if a gunner was not skilled at judging when the aiming marks were straddling a target.

This hint for gunners appears in the Tiger E tank manual:

"When a painter wants to measure exactly, he compares the size of the model with a pencil. You should compare the size of the graticule mark with the target! Then you will know how large your target is; you can measure its distance with the graticule marks."

Lieutenant Colonel Wilson M. Hawkins of the U.S. Army, commanding the 3rd Battalion, 67th Armored Regiment, expressed his opinion of German optical tank sights in a wartime report:

"The matter of tank gun sights has caused us much concern. I have looked through and worked with sights in German Mark V [Panther] and Mark VI [Tiger] tanks as well as our own. I find that the German sight has more magnifying power and clearness than our own, which is a big advantage to a gunner."

Sergeant Lewis A. Taylor of the U.S. Army's 2nd Armored Division, stated in a wartime report:

> The German telescopic sights mounted in their tanks are far superior to ours. In particular, it is more powerful. In fact all their optical equipment is superior to ours.

The Tiger B tanks fitted with Krupp/Porsche turrets featured an articulated binocular sighting system like the ones on many Tiger E tanks. The two openings in the front of the tank's turret for the binocular optical sighting system are clearly visible in this head-on photograph of a Tiger B tank fitted with a Krupp/Porsche turret. *Patton Museum*

TIGER TURRET TURNING RATES

The Tiger E and Tiger B tanks suffered a slight disadvantage in tank combat because their massive turrets resulted in sluggish turret slewing rates. It took a long time for the power traverse system to point the main gun in the direction of an enemy target. Extracts from a

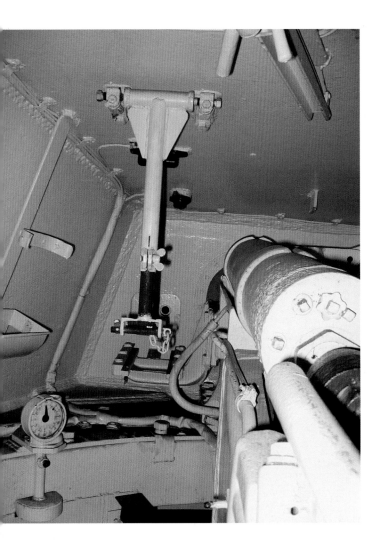

Inside the turret of a Tiger B tank with a Krupp/Henschel turret is the overhead bracket for attaching the articulated monocular sighting telescope that is missing from this vehicle. Where the telescope body should be sitting is the horizontal metal bracket for supporting it. To the lower left of the picture is the gunner's twelve-hour azimuth indicator. *Frank Shultz*

March 15, 1945, U.S. Army report define the traverse speed of the Tiger B tank turret.

General: Tests were made with a German PzKpfw Tiger Model B tank to determine the speed of traverse of the turret in relation to the engine speed.

Turret Traverse Mechanism: Since the turret is driven by the engine through a transfer case, the speed of the turret traverse is dependent upon the engine speed. A gearbox provides two ratios for controlling the speeds of traverse. Selection of the ratio to be used is made with a shift lever located on the left of the turret drive housing.

The traverse is controlled by two foot pedals located on the turret floor ahead of the gunner. The left pedal is used for left traverse and the right pedal for right traverse. The traverse can also be controlled by a hand lever connected to the foot pedal linkage. The lever is pushed down for right traverse and pulled up for left traverse. [This arrangement differs from the Tiger B tank examined by the British army described in chapter one because it lacks the gunner's tilting footplate traverse mechanism.]

A hand traverse wheel is also provided. Seven-hundred revolutions of the hand-wheel traverse the turret through 360 degrees.

Method of Testing: Before starting the time tests, the engine and gearing were warmed for 30 minutes. Engine temperature during the tests was 60°C. The time required for the turret to traverse 360 degrees was measured for engine speeds of 500, 1,000, 1,500, and 2,000 rpm for both the high and low ratio of the gearbox and for right and left traverse. In all cases, the turret was traversed from a standstill. Engine speeds in excess of 2,000 rpm were not used because of the possibility of damage to the engine.

Results: It was found that, with the engine turning over at 2000 rpm and with the high ratio engaged, the turret traversed 360 degrees in 19 seconds. With low ratio, the time required was 40 seconds.

British army test reports showed that the turret on the Tiger E tank also turned 360 degrees in nineteen seconds with its power traverse system set at the high ratio and with the engine speed at 2,000 revolutions per minute (rpm). With low engine speed (1,000 rpm) and with the power traverse system set at the low ratio, the turret took seventy-seven seconds to rotate 360 degrees.

BACKUP FIRE-CONTROL SYSTEMS

The Tiger gunner's firing accuracy improved with the aid of an illuminated clinometer on his right side. A clinometer is a device used to measure slopes. In artillery pieces and tank guns, the clinometer allows the gun crews to form a base for applying certain corrections in elevation in aiming the weapon or pointing it in the right elevation. The American military used quadrants rather than clinometers to measure slopes.

Being demonstrated is a small handheld stereoscopic rangefinder used by the crew of German 8.8cm FlaK guns. At some point in time, the thought arose that FlaK crews equipped with stereoscopic rangefinders might assist Tiger E tank crews in North Africa during combat. Although nothing came of it, the Germans had planned to mount stereoscopic rangefinders on Tiger B tanks before the war ended.
Michael Green

As a basic and crude aiming device, the Tiger E tank had a simple blade foresight mounted in front of the tank commander position. The Tiger B tank commander had access to a different system, which incorporated a small blade foresight fitted in front of his cupola. By dropping his head within the confines of his cupola, he could look out through a rear sight attached to the forward cupola periscope and quickly determine what his gunner was looking at (or should be looking at).

Some Tiger tank turrets came with a small scissor-like coincidence-type range finder stored within their turrets. When in use, it attached to the bottom interior of the tank commander's cupola on a movable bracket and projected out over the top of the cupola, allowing the tank commander to determine the range of distant targets while under armor protection. Wartime photographs also show German tank commanders holding the scissor-type optical range finder in their hands, as they looked out over the top of their cupolas.

A coincidence range finder displays the distance to the target after the tank commander aligns the erect image with an image in the field of view. The range then appears on a range scale. Coincidence-type range finders work well under conditions of clear visibility and for targets with sharply defined features. They are also easy to use, so extensive training is not necessary. Only a couple hours of instruction are usually required. On the minus side, they are ineffective at longer ranges or on targets having indistinct outlines.

In late 1942, the German army developed prototypes of a large, internally mounted stereoscopic range finder for the Tiger E, Tiger B, and a future version of the Panther tank. However, the war ended before the device went into production.

SECONDARY ARMAMENT

In addition to their 8.8cm main guns, the Tiger E and Tiger B tanks were fitted with several 7.92mm machine guns. Both Tiger models had a machine gun mounted alongside the main gun. In military terms, this is a coaxial machine gun or "coax." The Tiger E tank carried 5,250 rounds of 7.92mm ammunition for its coaxial machine gun, while the larger Tiger B tank had storage space for 5,850 rounds.

The Tiger tank's coaxial machine guns were employed against infantry and unarmored vehicles. This helped conserve the tank's main gun ammunition for tougher targets. The gunner on the Tiger tanks controlled the aiming and firing of the tank's coaxial machine gun with his power or manual traverse and elevation controls. The gunner fired the coaxial machine gun with a foot pedal located on the floor next to his right foot. The loader was responsible for both the loading and maintenance of the coaxial machine gun.

As with most World War II German tanks, both the Tiger E and Tiger B tanks had a front hull–mounted machine gun operated by the radioman, aimed by a simple telescope (the KZF 2), and fired by a hand trigger. The telescope gave the radioman a field of view of 18 degrees. The machine gun itself was breech-heavy and balanced by an equilibrator spring. In its ball mounting, this weapon could be elevated to 20 degrees and

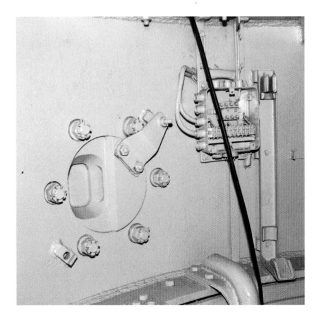

From the loader's position on an early production Tiger E tank, one of the vehicle's two pistol ports is visible. To the right of the pistol port is one of the tank's electrical system components. To the right of the electrical system component is a bracket for storing an MP40 submachine gun that the turret crew could fire through the pistol port if the need arose. *Andreas Kirchoff*

depressed 10 degrees. It had a traverse of 15 degrees both left and right. The Tiger E tank handbook describes the effectiveness of these weapons:

"Hull machine gun up to 200 meters against men, horses, and vehicles. Turret machine gun up to 400 meters against men, horses, and vehicles. If there's a lot of them, then at greater ranges. Also for occupied houses and for enemy soldiers lying prone on the ground."

The Tiger E tank with the late-model cupola and the Tiger B tank were equipped with an attachment rail on the commander's cupola for the mounting of an additional 7.92mm machine gun. Because this weapon was independent of the Tiger tank's main gun and coaxial machine gun, the tank commander could engage a second target at the same time his gunner was firing at the first. Like the coaxial gun, it was useful for firing at infantry or unarmored vehicles.

The 7.92mm machine guns mounted in the Tiger tanks were the vehicle-mounted versions of the well-known German *Maschinegewehr* 34 (MG34). First accepted for German army service in 1934, the MG34 did not reach production until 1936.

Berent Isenberg recalls that they never mounted the MG34 machine gun on any of their unit's Tiger E tanks with the late-model tank commander's cupolas. In fact, they never used any of their machine guns during his time in Italy, as they depended on the long-range accuracy of their 8.8cm main gun to keep the enemy at such a distance they never needed to fire their onboard machine guns.

In addition to the crew's individual pistols, most Tiger turrets mounted a single MP38 or MP40 model submachine gun, incorrectly known to most Allied soldiers as the *Schmeisser;* it was nicknamed the "Burp gun" by many Allied soldiers. Tiger tank crews used it for guard duty if there was no infantry support or as a close-in defense weapon of last resort.

There were two large and elaborate small-arm (pistol) ports in the earliest versions of the Tiger E tank turret. This soon dropped to one as a new loader's rear escape hatch took over the spot once occupied by one of the small-arms ports. The small-arms ports opened and closed by rotating an internally mounted armor shutter. In an effort to speed up production and keep costs down, the elaborate small-arms port on the left side of the turret (for the tank commander's use) was replaced by a simple armored plug in July 1943.

The Krupp turrets for the failed Porsche Tiger B contender were originally fitted with a single small gun port on the left side, which was later plugged.

Beginning in January 1943, all Tiger E tanks coming off the assembly lines featured an antipersonnel mine discharger system referred to in German as the *Minenabwurfvorrichtung.* This infantry antipersonnel weapons system consisted of five small single-shot S-mine dischargers. One unit was mounted in each corner of the hull and the fifth was located halfway along the left side of the hull. The command variant of the Tiger E tank had only four—one in each corner.

The *Minenabwurfvorrichtung* on Tiger E tanks disappeared in October 1943, replaced by a more versatile system known as the *Nahverteidigungswaffe* ("close defense weapon"). It was a breech-loaded, singe-shot, multipurpose, 360-degree rotating antipersonnel grenade launcher mounted in the roof of the Tiger E tank turret that also fired smoke grenades or signaling flares. The loader operated the grenade launcher from within the vehicle. Owing to production delays, it did not appear on all new Tiger E tanks until March 1944. The *Nahverteidigungswaffe* also appeared on many Tiger B tanks.

This picture shows a Krupp/Henschel turret roof. Visible on the roof of the vehicle's turret is the small circular exterior opening, just behind the loader's hatch, for the small traversable breech-loading mortar attached to the turret roof of the tank. Also visible is the loader's front turret-mounted periscope and the upper portion of the turret exhaust ventilation fan. *Patton Museum*

WEAPON-ARMED VARIANTS OF THE TIGER TANKS

Due to combat experience gained during the street-to-street fighting for the Soviet city of Stalingrad in 1942, the German army saw a need for a special-purpose, heavily armored assault vehicle that could effectively destroy enemy defensive fortifications at close range with a single shot. The original weapon chosen for the role was a 210mm howitzer, however; the howitzer was not available when needed, so a 380mm (15-inch) breech-

Not too long after the production of the Tiger E tank began, an escape hatch (seen here) for the loader replaced one of the two pistol ports in the vehicle's turret. On later versions of the Tiger E tank, a small 360 degree traversable breech-loading mortar mounted in the turret roof and firing antipersonnel projectiles appeared at the loader's position, as seen in this picture. *Franck Schulz*

On display at a German military museum is an example of an odd-looking vehicle armed with a large breech-loaded mortar that fired a rocket-assisted projectile weighing more than seven hundred pounds to a distance of almost four miles. The Germans mounted this weapon on the chassis of a Tiger E tank. *Michael Green*

loaded mortar, firing rocket-assisted projectiles, appeared in its place.

Because of the great weight and size of the large mortar and its rocket-assisted rounds, a decision came down to mount it on the chassis of the Tiger E tank. The normal superstructure and turret of the vehicle disappeared; replaced by a heavy rectangular armored box with a 45-degree sloping front plate that was six inches thick. Each vehicle had storage space for twelve rounds, either HE or shaped charge. Only eighteen of these sixty-four-ton vehicles rolled off the production line between August and December 1944. To the German army, the vehicle was called the "*Sturmmorser* ("assault mortar") Tiger." The troops often referred to it as the *Sturmtiger* or *Sturmpanzer* VI.

A gun-armed variant that appeared on a lengthened chassis of the Tiger B tank, beginning in July 1944, was the *Jagdtiger* ("hunting tiger"). It mounted in a nonrotating armored casemate, with limited traverse and elevation, one of two versions of a 128mm gun, with a length of about twenty-three feet. The guns fired a roughly sixty-two-pound APCBC projectile at a muzzle velocity of 3,020 feet per second. There was also an HE round for the gun. Due to the size and weight of the complete round, at more than one hundred pounds, the *Jagdtiger* featured separate loading ammunition. The vehicle had storage space for thirty-eight projectiles and thirty-eight metal cartridge cases.

The *Jagdtiger* turned out to be the heaviest production armored fighting vehicle built during World War II,

The massive bulk of the badly underpowered Jagdtiger is evident in this picture. The 12.8cm main gun resides in a heavily armored casemate mounted on the chassis of a Tiger B tank. Because the vehicle lacked a traversable turret, aiming the main gun at something other than right in front of it meant turning the entire vehicle. *Michael Green*

coming in at more than 77.3 tons, according to a U.S. Army wartime report. The vehicle was just a bit over nine feet tall and about twenty-six feet long when excluding the gun. With the gun included, the *Jagdtiger* reached forty feet in length. The frontal armor on the vehicle's superstructure was sloped at 15 degrees and was almost ten inches thick, not counting the gun shield that ranged in thickness from a little more than two up to five inches.

Of the 150 *Jagdtiger*s ordered by the German army, only seventy-seven made it off the assembly before the war in Europe ended. Two of the seventy-seven *Jagdtiger*s built were mounted on the suspension system of the passed-over Porsche Tiger B tank prototype. The vehicle's crew consisted of six men: driver, radioman, tank commander, gunner, and two loaders due to the separate loading ammunition.

Otto Carius spent the last few weeks of World War II in command of a company of *Jagdtiger*s. In the following passage, he describes his impressions of the vehicle.

When the assault guns were calibrated in Sennelager, we experienced our first failure. Despite its 82 tons, our Hunting Tiger didn't want to act like we wanted it to. Only its armor was satisfactory; its maneuverability left a lot to be desired. In addition, it was an assault gun. There was no traversing turret, just an enclosed armored housing. Any large traversing of the main gun had to done by moving the entire vehicle. Because of that, transmission and steering differentials soon broke down. That such a monstrosity had to be constructed in the final phase of the war made no sense at all.

To the left of this Tiger E tank's 8.8cm main gun is the opening in the gun shield for the coaxial 7.92mm machine gun. On the right of the main gun are the two small openings for the gunner's binocular telescopic sight. This early model Tiger E tank lacks the thickening around the gun sight openings that began appearing on new production vehicles in November 1942. *Thomas Anderson*

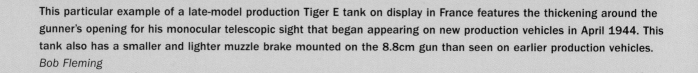

This particular example of a late-model production Tiger E tank on display in France features the thickening around the gunner's opening for his monocular telescopic sight that began appearing on new production vehicles in April 1944. This tank also has a smaller and lighter muzzle brake mounted on the 8.8cm gun than seen on earlier production vehicles. *Bob Fleming*

CHAPTER THREE
PROTECTION

Effective range for a tank gun is analogous to a boxer's reach. Possessing an effective weapon that outreaches your opponent's is a big advantage in any fight. It allows you to hammer him before he can close with you. However, in battles there are always occasions when the enemy's tanks are able to get close enough to your tank to employ their shorter-range weapons on your vehicle, thus nullifying your long-range firepower advantage.

Dug-in and hidden towed antitank guns, whose preferred tactic is the close-in ambush, were a significant threat faced by tankers during World War II. In an ideal world, you would always know where and when your enemy was about to strike and adapt your tactics so as not to take a hit. In the real world, however, no amount of planning can prevent the enemy from scoring hits at least some of the time. To survive such encounters requires armor protection. The major disadvantage of armor protection has always been weight.

A good tank design is a compromise of armor protection, firepower, mobility, and reliability. Overemphasis in any one area can ruin battlefield effectiveness. The Germans chose to emphasize firepower and protection over mobility and reliability in the Tiger design. However, no one tank can ever carry enough armor to completely protect itself from any battlefield threat, so a tank's armor is always heaviest in places where it is most likely to be hit.

World War II tank designers used common sense in deciding where to place the thickest armor, reasoning that a tank would usually be faced toward an enemy. This position minimized the visual silhouette, protected the suspension, and the crew and turret would be pointed toward incoming fire. Postwar studies based on historical experience confirmed that the heaviest armor should go on a 60-degree frontal arc of the hull and the turret.

TIGER E TANK ARMOR

For maximum armor protection, the tank's lower hull and the portion of the hull projecting above the suspension system (referred to as the *superstructure*) was constructed of flat rolled homogenous armor (RHA) plates joined together by overlapping stepped welded joints dovetailed together for both mechanical strength and armor performance.

RHA offers some advantages over face-hardened armor and cast homogenous armor (CHA) because it is easier to produce in large quantities and welds easily into a vehicle structure. Homogenous means that the material has the same characteristics throughout its thickness. The rolling process hardens the material and ensures consistent

An early production Tiger E tank is about to have its turret fitted on the Henschel production line. The gun shields on the front of tank turrets tend to have the thickest armor on the vehicle, because it is the most likely spot struck in battle by enemy projectiles, given the fact that the crew of any given tank will keep that part of the tank facing the enemy as much as possible. *Patton Museum*

properties from batch to batch so that armor performance was guaranteed for a given thickness of RHA.

RHA also offered superior protection when struck by antitank projectiles due to its ductility, which is the property of a material that allows it to withstand large amounts of deformation before fracturing. It also does well in protecting against the shock waves generated by large-caliber projectiles striking the exterior of a tank's armor, as well as the blast from high-explosive (HE) projectiles. A major disadvantage of RHA is its difficulty to form easily.

A definition of the term *shock* in the context of tank armor comes from a postwar U.S. Army report:

> The term "shock" refers, in general, to a sudden change in motion of a mechanical system and is concerned with the magnitude and the duration of the forces developed. A sharp blow on a steel plate will cause the plate to act like an extremely flexible membrane, and to vibrate back and forth like a drumhead. The vibration is generally composed of superimposed vibrations of several frequencies. The high frequency vibrations will generally have small displacements and high accelerations, while the lower frequencies are generally associated with the large displacements and lower accelerations.

In this illustration, the thickest of many parts of early- and mid-production Tiger E tank hulls and turrets are listed in millimeters. The height of the original tank commander's cupola fitted to the Tiger E tank was a serious design error and was later corrected on subsequent production vehicles with a much lower profile cupola, beginning in July 1943. *James D. Brown*

The Red Army placed very little effort in the development of man-portable antitank weapons for its infantry units during World War II. Instead of rocket launchers, like the famous American bazooka, Red Army soldiers had to depend on large 14.5mm antitank rifles similar to the one shown. While firing too small a projectile to destroy a Tiger tank, they could do serious damage to the vehicle's vision devices. *Patton Museum*

The Tiger E superstructure at the front of the vehicle consisted of a near-vertical RHA plate more than four inches thick and sloped at an angle of 10 degrees. The RHA plate located directly below and in front of it was sloped at 80 degrees and was about two and a half inches thick. The hull nose plate at the lower front was a bit more than four inches thick and sloped at 24 degrees.

The armor thickness on the Tiger E tank's vertical superstructure side plates was just over three inches, while the vertical hull plates located behind the suspension system were two and a half inches thick. The rear engine plate was also a bit over three inches thick and sloped at 8 degrees. The superstructure roof plate and the bottom hull plate of the Tiger E tank were an inch thick.

The Tiger E tank's horseshoe-shaped turret consisted of a single RHA plate (with curved and straight sections) a little more than three inches thick. To make room for the gunner and his controls on the left side of the turret, the turret was slightly asymmetric by about four inches on the left side.

The roof of the Tiger E turret was originally about an inch thick. Because combat experience demonstrated that it could not resist penetration from large-caliber HE

artillery rounds, the builder increased it to almost two inches, starting in March 1944.

At the front of the Tiger E tank turret was a very large CHA gun shield, referred to as a mantlet by the British. A description of it appears in a British army report dated September 1943:

> The thickness of the mantlet, measured through the gun sight holes is 150mm [six inches], in the central portion; where the front plate is reinforced around the gun, the thickness is approximately 205mm [about eight inches]. These thicknesses of over 100mm [four inches] are only local and [are] thought that the protection afforded by the mantlet as a whole would be greater than given by a plate of uniform thickness of 100mm.

An external thickening of the gunner's sight holes in the gun shield of the Tiger E tank came up for discussion in March 1942 and began appearing on new production tanks in November 1942. This brought the armor thickness around the gunner's sight holes up to about seven inches on Tiger E tanks.

The driver of a Tiger E tank examines the damage inflicted on the front superstructure plate by an AP projectile that failed to penetrate the armor just in front of his position. Such a strike in described in military terms as a partial penetration. Penetration is complete when any portion of a projectile protrudes through armor plate. *Patton Museum*

Traditionally, tank designers employ CHA because of its almost limitless formability. For this reason, it has historically been used for the complex shapes of tank gun shields and turrets. One advantage of using CHA is the reduced manufacturing costs of preparing and welding thick sections of armor steel plate with ballistic-quality welds. A disadvantage of CHA is its lower ductility and toughness because it is not work-hardened like RHA. Another disadvantage is the difficulty of avoiding casting porosity (gas bubble inclusions) and other flaws that can locally diminish armor performance.

OPINIONS ON THE TIGER E TANK ARMOR

German army tank ace Otto Carius stated his opinion of the quality of the steel armor on his Tiger E tank in his 1960 book titled *Tiger im Schlamm (Tiger in the Mud):*

> Again and again, we admired the quality of the steel on our tanks. It was hard without being brittle. Despite its hardness, it was also very elastic. If an antitank round didn't hit the tank's armor plate dead on, it would slide off on its side and leave behind a gouge as if you had run your finger over a soft piece of butter.

Another example of the effectiveness of the armor protection on the Tiger E tank appears in some passages from a report by a German lieutenant fighting in Russia. The translated text appears in the book titled *Panzer Truppen 2: The Complete Guide to the Creation and Combat Employment of Germany's Tank Force: 1943–1945,* edited by Thomas L. Jentz.

> On 10 and 11 February 1943 in an attack on the collective farm west of Sserernikowo, battle group Sander faced greatly superior forces. The Tigers in the lead platoon drew most of the enemy fire on themselves. The fire came mostly from the right flank and the front from tanks, anti-tank guns, and infantry with anti-tank rifles, all opening fire at the longest range possible.
>
> At the beginning of the attack, my Tiger was hit on the front of the superstructure by a 7.62cm [76mm] anti-tank gun. The track links, which had been fastened to the superstructure front plate by a steel bar, were shot away. We heard a dull clang and felt a slight jolt inside the Tiger. At the same time, we observed many near misses striking the ground to the front and the side of the Tiger.
>
> Shortly thereafter, I received a hit on the commander's cupola from a 4.5cm [45mm] anti-tank gun. The brackets holding the glass vision block flew off. The block became welded tight but visibility was eliminated by the impact of the shell fragments. A second hit on the cupola knocked brackets loose from the turret ceiling. At the same time, a heat wave and a cloud of acrid smoke enveloped the crew. Two hits from 4.5cm anti-tank shells and 15 hits from anti-tank rounds were counted on the cupola after the battle.

Like the Red Army, the British army fielded a variety of towed antitank guns, one of the most successful being the seventeen-pounder, as shown here on its split trail carriage. The first examples went off to North Africa to deal with the German Tiger E tanks sent there. Due to the weight of the gun and carriage, the British army soon began mounting it on a variety of armored tracked vehicles. *Michael Green*

The loader's hatch, somewhat stuck and therefore about half open, received several hits from anti-tank rifles which knocked some brackets off. Other rounds striking the hatch jammed the hinges so that it could be opened only with the aid of a wrecking bar after the battle. . . . After another 7.62cm anti-tank shell struck the gun mantle, the brackets holding the gun snapped, the recoil cylinder began losing fluid, and the gun remained at full recoil. The shaking caused by additional hits damaged the radio, a gas tube, and the gear lever by the driver. The engine caught fire when the shield protecting the exhaust muffler was shot away, but the fire was rapidly extinguished.

An explosive charge thrown on top of the Tiger from the side was sensed as a dull explosion accompanied by heat and smoke enveloping the Tiger and the crew.

We counted 227 hits from anti-tank rifle rounds, 14 hits from 5.7cm [57mm] and 4.5cm anti-tank guns, and 11 hits from 7.62cm guns. The right track and suspension were heavily damaged. Several road wheels and their suspension arms were perforated. The idler wheel had worked out of its mount. In spite of all this damage, the Tiger still managed to cover an additional 60 kilometers under its own power.

RED ARMY ANTITANK RIFLES

The 14.5mm Soviet army antitank rifles used against the Tiger tanks in this account were either the manually operated single-shot PRTD-41 or the gas-operated semi-automatic PTRS-41 with a five-round magazine. Soviet factories built about 185,000 PRTD-41s and 63,000 PTRS-41s during World War II. Both bipod-mounted weapons measured more than six feet long and were operated by a crew of two. The PRTD-41 weighed thirty-eight pounds

The turret wall of a Tiger E tank, on the loader's side of the tank, has taken numerous large-caliber hits from AP projectiles. The strikes on the upper portion of the tank's turret buckled the turret roof plate, while the lowest hit on the turret wall fractured the armor along a horizontal seam. *Patton Museum*

and the PTRS-41 weighed forty-six pounds. The 14.5mm steel- or tungsten-cored projectiles had a muzzle velocity of 3,314 feet per second and could penetrate about an inch of armor at 550 yards.

While the Red Army antitank rifles obviously could not destroy a Tiger tank, they could do serious damage to the periscope, vision blocks, and other external components. This German army report describes the battle damage suffered by a Tiger E tank battalion:

> The Russian Model 42 antitank rifle obtained penetrations of up to 17mm [a little more than half an inch] on the front slope in front of the driver's position. This rifle was encountered quite often and can be spotted by its prominent muzzle flash. In one case, an oblique hit was made against the forward vision slit of the tank commander's cupola. Its corner broke

off and ricocheted, making the vision block unusable—the result of a direct hit, with a probable penetration. The rounds of the antitank rifle usually strike in the vicinity of the vision slots.

ALLIED ENCOUNTERS WITH TIGER E TANK ARMOR

The U.S. Army first encountered the Tiger E tank in Tunisia, North Africa, in February 1943, when elements of the 1st Armored Division had the misfortune of engaging the German army's *Schwere Heeres Panzer Abteilung* ("army heavy tank battalion") 501. Battalion 501 had arrived in Tunisia with 20 Tiger E tanks in November 1942. (The appellation *army* in the unit name distinguishes it from Waffen SS forces, which were also equipped with tanks.) After this engagement, the Tiger E tanks left many American tanks destroyed and burning on the battlefield. While the German tankers also took losses, the Tiger E tanks would remain a serious threat to the U.S. Army fighting in North Africa throughout the war.

In 1943, the British army interviewed a captured German Tiger E tank gunner in which he compared the effectiveness of the Tiger armor protection levels with the Panzer III and IV medium tanks he had served on before:

> His [the gunner's] confidence has been fully restored since he transferred to Tiger tanks. On every occasion, he stresses the great feeling of security that a crew has inside an AFV [armored fighting vehicle] with armor. Crews feel very certain of their ability to engage any target. He claims that he once ran into fire from the flank from seven 17-pounder antitank guns at close range and having turned the hull of his tank so that a three-quarter view was presented to the fire, he proceeded to destroy five out of seven antitank guns with HE rounds. Several hits were registered on the frontal armor of the Tiger but penetration was not achieved. Deep dents only resulted, with flaking from shell splinters.

A U.S. War Department Intelligence Bulletin dated January 1945 includes the following description of a combat encounter by a New Zealand Division with a Tiger E tank in Italy:

> A Tiger was observed about 3,000 yards away, engaging three Shermans. When it set one of the

It was British army six-pounder (57mm) towed antitank guns, like the one shown here, that accounted for the first German Tiger E tanks destroyed in North Africa on January 20, 1943. This weapon showed up in the field in late 1941 and fired a roughly six-pound projectile that could penetrate almost three inches of armor at one thousand yards. *Michael Green*

Shermans afire, the other two withdrew over a crest. A 17-pounder [towed British Army 76.2mm antitank gun] was brought up to within 2,400 yards of the Tiger, and engaged it from a flank. When the Tiger realized that it was being engaged by a high-velocity gun it swung around 90 degrees so that its heavy frontal armor was toward the gun. In the ensuing duel, one round hit the turret, another round hit the suspension, and two near-short rounds probably ricocheted into the tank. The tank was not put out of action. The range was too great to expect a kill; hence, the New Zealanders' tactics were to make the Tiger expose its flank to the Shermans at a range of almost 500 yards, by swinging around onto the antitank gun. The Tiger did just this, and, when it was engaged by the Shermans, it withdrew. The enemy infantry protection of half a dozen to a dozen men was engaged by machine guns.

Discovered in North Africa, a weak spot of the Tiger E tank proved to be the exterior portion of the turret ring guide, which was subject to jamming when struck from overlooking positions by projectiles or artillery fragments. To correct this, all new Tiger E tanks coming off the assembly lines after February 1944 came with a turret ring guard that bolted to the superstructure roof plate.

An added protection feature to Tiger E tank turrets, beginning in August 1942, consisted of two sets of smoke grenade launchers, each consisting of three cylinder-like tubes, mounted on either side of the vehicle's turret. The Tiger E tank crew fired the smoke grenade launchers from within the confines of the vehicle's turret. They disappeared from the Tiger E tanks beginning in February 1943, due to reports that small-arms fire had set them off, and the resulting smoke had made it impossible for the struck tank's crew to function.

AMERICAN AND BRITISH HANDHELD ANTITANK WEAPONS

The best-known handheld antitank weapon used by American soldiers during World War II was the roughly thirteen-pound bazooka. The original version was

The American M1 2.36-inch Bazooka, pictured here, was a rocket-firing weapon, with a small shaped charge warhead that gave the average infantryman at least a chance of destroying enemy armored vehicles, Tiger tanks being a little iffy. The problem was that to be effective, a soldier had to be at close range to the intended target, which left him vulnerable to enemy counter fire. *Michael Green*

In this U.S. Army wartime training picture of a two-man bazooka team, the soldier in the rear is inserting the shaped charged–equipped rocket into the rear of the long metal tube that made up the weapon. With the rocket hooked up to the electrical firing system, the loader would tap the soldier holding the bazooka on the helmet to let him know that he could fire the weapon. *National Archives*

The PIAT (projector, infantry, antitank) Mk 1 employed by the British army during World War II, fired a small shaped charge warhead, which on lucky occasions might penetrate the armor of a Tiger tank. Rather than using a rocket motor as a delivery method, the PIAT employed coiled spring energy. *Michael Green*

designated the Launcher, Rocket, 2.36-inch, M1. Invented by Colonel Skinner of the U.S. Army, the bazooka fired a 2.36-inch-diameter rocket that weighed about three and a half pounds and featured a shaped charge warhead.

In theory, the shaped charge warhead on the bazooka rocket could penetrate almost five inches of armor. Tests conducted by the U.S. Army 702nd Tank Destroyer Battalion in western Europe between July and November 1944 proved otherwise:

> The bazooka could not penetrate the front of the Mark V (Panther) or Mark VI (Tiger) tanks nor the side of the Mark VI, but could penetrate the side and turret of the Mark V.

A U.S. Army Ordnance observer claimed that an American bazooka destroyed a Tiger E tank with a lucky hit to the driver's vision slot during the fighting for Sicily in 1943. Because of the very short one-hundred-yard effective range of the bazooka, very few American soldiers were willing to stand in front of a German tank to do this again.

The British army and its Commonwealth Allies fielded a three-foot-long handheld antitank weapon known as the projector, infantry, anti-tank (PIAT). Unlike the bazooka, which fired a small rocket armed with a shaped charge warhead, the thirty-two-pound PIAT was nothing more than a hollow tube with a firing spring (cocked by hand before the first shot) and a long steel rod. When the oper-

As a quick countermeasure to the fielding of the Tiger E tank, the Red Army took the chassis of the less than successful KV-1 heavy tank and turned it into a turretless self-propelled assault gun armed with a 152mm gun/howitzer that fired projectiles large enough to punch through the armor on Tiger tanks. This photograph of an SU-152 comes from a German army report. *Patton Museum*

The Red Army decided to phase out the troublesome KV-1 heavy tank from service and replace it with the much superior IS-II heavy tank, armed with a 122mm main gun. They also decided to use the IS-II chassis as the base for a new and improved turretless assault gun designated the ISU-152, seen here on display at a Russian army tank museum. *Vladimir Yakubov*

ator pulled the weapon's trigger, a spring pushed the steel rod forward, hurling a three-pound projectile (armed with a shaped charge warhead) through the air toward a target. The bomb itself was fitted with a tail, which contained a small propelling charge that went off when hit by the steel rod. The force of the propelling charge pushed the steel rod and spring back to the cocked position so the operator could quickly reload and fire another round.

In theory, the PIAT shaped charge warhead could penetrate up to four inches of armor. However, combat experience showed that it could not do this consistently. British factories produced about 115,000 units of the weapon during World War II.

RED ARMY SOLUTIONS FOR THE TIGER E TANK

After capturing their first Tiger E tank in January 1943, the Red Army set about testing the armor protection levels on the vehicle. To their dismay, they discovered that none of their main tank guns could destroy a Tiger E tank. As a quick fix, the Red Army mounted a variety of large antiair-

Another turretless Red Army self-propelled assault gun that appeared in World War II and saw use against Tiger tanks was the SU-122 assault howitzer. Armed with a 122mm howitzer and mounted on the chassis of the T34 medium tank, its primary role was in direct fire-support of an infantry unit. However, it did carry a shaped charge round whose projectile could penetrate more than eight inches of armor at 688 yards and therefore posed a threat to Tiger tanks. *Patton Museum*

Also mounted on the chassis of the T34 medium tank was the SU-100, armed with a modified 100mm naval gun, firing fixed ammunition that could penetrate the armor on German Tiger tanks. It first appeared in Red Army service in late 1944. More than 1,500 units of the SU-100 came off Russian assembly lines before World War II ended. *Michael Green*

The Red Army T34/85 medium tank began appearing in Red Army service in early 1944 and mounted an excellent 85mm main gun that could penetrate the armor on German Tiger tanks from the sides and rear. Due to its larger and heavier main gun, as well as slightly thicker armor, the T34/85 was a bit slower and had less range than the T34/76 medium tank. *Michael Green*

craft guns and artillery pieces on turretless tanks (referred to as *Samokhodnaya Ustanovka* (SU), or self-propelled gun systems. Because there was no turret, the main guns faced forward with limited traverse and elevation capability.

Many German tankers who served on the Eastern Front during World War II considered the Red Army SUs more dangerous than any of their wartime tanks or towed antitank guns. In a 1949 article published by *Armor Cavalry Journal*, Soviet weapons expert Garrett Underhill described the official Red Army wartime view of their SUs:

> The Soviets have stated that for antitank and assault gun infantry support work they preferred the SU's lower silhouette and larger gun. The silhouette afforded greater security through concealment, enabling surprise action. It also presented a smaller target to antitank guns. The gun affords greater hitting power at maximum ranges, as well as more devastating HE effects against infantry weapons.

The best-known Red Army SU from World War II turned out to be the forty-five-ton SU-152 based on the chassis of the KV heavy tank. The Russians called it the *Zveroboy*, or beast killer, and the vehicle first saw action against German tanks in July 1943.

An improved version of the SU-152, based on the chassis of the IS-2 Stalin heavy tank, entered into production at the end of 1943. It was designated ISU-152. When used in the tank destroyer role, it took on the name of its predecessor, *Zveroboy*, owing to its effectiveness in killing German Panther, Tiger, and other German tanks named for predatory animals.

The ISU-152 was similar in overall appearance to the SU-152 but featured a new gun shield and thicker frontal armor. Both vehicles had a four-man crew and room for only twenty main gun rounds. Both versions used the M37 152mm gun, which was twelve feet long and fired an AP or HE round that weighed more than

Pictured on display at a Russian army tank museum is this example of a Red Army IS-2 Stalin heavy tank, armed with a 122mm main gun. It proved to be their first tank that was on roughly equal terms in armor protection and firepower with the Tiger tanks. The crews of German Tiger tanks received instructions to shoot at IS-2 tanks first, due to the threat they posed to their own tanks. *Vladimir Yakubov*

An 85mm AP round from a Red Army T-34/85 medium tank appears on the far right of this picture. In the center of the picture is an AP round fired from the 7.5cm gun mounted on the Panther medium tank. On the far left is an AP round fired from the 8.8cm gun on the Tiger B tank. The larger the cartridge case, the more propellant, the higher the muzzle velocity. *Michael Green*

one hundred pounds. What the projectiles from these rounds lacked in muzzle velocity (less than two thousand feet per second), they made up for in projectile mass. The AP ML-20 projectile could penetrate more than four inches of armor at a range of 2,200 yards.

Due to a shortage of the M37 guns for the ISU-152, the Red Army began mounting the D-25S 122mm gun on a turretless chassis of the IS-2 Stalin heavy tank and referred to it as the ISU-122.

The SU-85 was another Red Army SU used against the Tiger E tank. Armed with a D-5T 85mm gun, the twenty-nine-ton assault gun came off the factory floor in the middle of 1943. It fired a twenty-pound AP projectile at a muzzle velocity of 2,600 feet per second.

In February 1944, the ZIS S-53 85mm gun was mounted in a new and larger cast-armor three-man turret and was installed on the T34 medium tank chassis. This combination became the T34/85 medium tank. Although the main gun on the T34/85 could not penetrate the frontal armor array of the Tiger tanks, it could penetrate the sides and rear armor of the Tiger tank at certain ranges.

At this point in the war, the Red Army also mounted a D-10S 100mm main gun on the SU-85 chassis. This new thirty-one-ton vehicle received the designation SU-100.

The D-10S barrel length was about eighteen feet. The sixty-six-pound APCBC round had a projectile weight of thirty-four pounds. Muzzle velocity was 2,950

In contrast to the flat vertical armor surfaces on the Tiger E tank, the designers of the Tiger B tank did their best to slope every surface on the vehicle's hull and turret, as is evident in this picture of a Tiger B tank. Well-sloped armor increases the ability to resist penetration because the chances of an AP projectile glancing off dramatically increase. *David Marian*

feet per second. Both the SU-85 and SU-100 featured a three-inch-thick gun shield with an additional inch of armor thickness on portions directly facing the threat.

In December 1942, the Red Army fielded another turretless SU based on the T34 chassis. The SU-122 was armed with an M38 122mm main gun that fired a fifty-six-pound APCBC projectile or a forty-eight-pound HE projectile. Although the M38 gun was capable of destroying Tiger tanks, the SU-122 normally served in the direct fire-support role for Red Army infantry units.

RED ARMY COUNTERPART TO THE TIGER E TANK

The IS-2, or Stalin heavy tank, was the first Red Army tank to be on somewhat even terms with the Tiger E tank. The nomenclature IS stands for Joseph Stalin's initials (*I* is Stalin's first initial in Russian). The IS-2 weighed roughly forty-six tons and was operated by four men. The armor was six inches thick at the front of the turret.

The main armament was a D-25T 122mm gun with a double-baffle muzzle brake at the end of the nineteen-foot-long barrel. The round weighed eighty-six and a half pounds, with a projectile portion that weighed fifty-five pounds. Muzzle velocity was 2,600 feet per second.

Because of the huge size of the rounds, the vehicle could carry only twenty-eight main gun rounds.

Unlike the one-piece (fixed) main gun rounds fired from the Tiger tanks, the IS-Stalin tank's weapon derived from an artillery design where the projectile and propellant are loaded separately. It would have been relatively easy to adapt a fixed cartridge, but the resulting round would have been too heavy for a loader to handle rapidly, and too long to manipulate within the confines of the vehicle. This slowed down the gun's rate of fire as the projectile went in first followed by the metal cartridge case. Except for the SU-85 and the SU-100, all of the Red Army's large SUs fired separately loaded main gun rounds.

The first IS-2 rolled off the assembly lines in February 1944 and saw action against Tiger E tanks that April. The IS-2 was so effective against German tanks that Tiger crews received instructions to destroy IS-2 tanks before engaging any other targets. German general Hasso Von Manteuffel considered the IS-2 the best tank of World War II. The Red Army fielded about three thousand five hundred IS-2 tanks before the war in Europe ended.

Despite some successes in service against German tanks, a German Tiger tank battalion commander's

When an AP projectile strikes the sloped front armor of a tank at a horizontal angle, like this Tiger B tank pictured, it creates extreme bending stresses, which tend to break it up transversely. When an AP projectile strikes a flat vertical armor surface, the projectile finds itself subjected to compressive stress that leaves the nose of the projectile intact and the projectile body breaking up into numerous pieces. *Andreas Kirchoff*

thoughts on the IS-2 Stalin tank appeared in a British army report:

> Most Stalin tanks will withdraw on encountering Tigers without attempting to engage in a firefight. Stalin tanks generally open fire at ranges over 2,200 yards and then only if standing oblique to the target. Enemy crews tend to abandon tanks as soon as hit.

TIGER B TANK ARMOR ARRANGEMENT

Unlike the Tiger E tank, with its generally flat, boxlike, RHA armored hull and superstructure, the first prototype of the Tiger B tank featured sloped RHA plates interlocked with stepped welded joints. This derived from the success of the Panther medium tank's sloped armor arrangement. The similarity to the Panther's hull shape resulted in many U.S. Army technical intelligence reports referring to the first Tiger B tanks captured as scaled up Panther tanks.

Russians and Germans adopted sloped armor for their tanks because sloping surfaces increased its effective thickness when measured from a horizontal plane (a measurement known as the armor basis). Also, penetration became more difficult because projectiles are more likely to deflect than penetrate.

The six-inch-thick front hull/superstructure plate (also known as the glacis) of the Tiger B tank was sloped at 50 degrees. The four-inch-thick hull nose plate, just below the glacis plate, was sloped at 55 degrees. The upper side superstructure plates were three inches thick and sloped at 25 degrees. The lower hull side plates (necessarily vertical) were also three inches thick. The Tiger B armored top superstructure plate was an inch and a half thick, as was the bottom hull plate. The rear plate sloped at 25 degrees and was three inches thick.

Extracts from a U.S. Army report point out the importance of the armor thickness arrangement of tank hulls and the slope (obliquity) of their armor.

> Naturally, one of the first considerations in the apportionment of the total armor weight will be how much is allowed for each component of the vehicle. The heaviest attack against an armored vehicle will, of course, be borne by its front, and, therefore, the greatest thickness of hull armor should usually be applied to its front. The next greatest protection should be afforded by the sides, roof, floor, and rear in that order, as the extent of attack in various areas will generally vary according to that sequence.

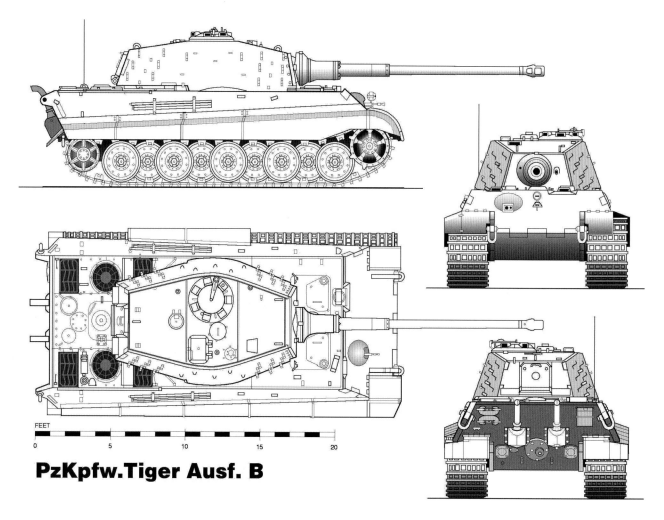

PzKpfw.Tiger Ausf. B

A four-view line illustration shows the various features of the Tiger B tank equipped with the Krupp/Henschel turret. The sloping of tank armor plate can effectively almost double the ballistic protection afforded an armored vehicle.
George Bradford

Obliquities at which the various plates are to be placed are very important and should be selected carefully, remembering the need for equalization of protection. . . .

The British have conducted a number of investigations of the application of obliquity to armored vehicle design. They point out that frontal armor of a vehicle should be designed to be invulnerable to the heaviest attack the vehicle is expected to encounter. Such a practice will greatly increase the protection afforded since it has been indicated that about 40 percent of all hits on tanks in World War II were located on the frontal areas. An invulnerable frontal area will increase a vehicle's chance of survival,

significantly. Tests made by the British show that for best protection against APC projectiles [referred to by the British as APCBC projectiles] the armor obliquity should be between 50 degrees and 70 degrees with a preference nearer to 50 than 70 degrees. Against attack of tungsten-carbide-cored projectiles they found that an obliquity of 60 degrees or more would afford optimum protection.

Sloped tank armor provides a dramatic increase in protection from horizontal strikes by AP projectiles when compared to vertical armor plate. An example of this appears in a statement by 2nd Lt. Robert V. McQuillen in a wartime U.S. Army report:

The curved front turret armor plate seen on this Tiger B tank marks it as one of the Krupp turrets originally ordered for the failed Porsche chassis candidate for a new heavy tank. The curve came about in order to make the frontal turret area as small a target as possible. While done with the right intentions, the turret designers created a shot trap under the bottom of the tank's gun shield. *Patton Museum*

We were fired on by three German Mark VI [Tiger B] tanks and had three mediums knocked out; two of them burned. The German tanks were spotted and our mediums returned the fire and succeeded in driving off two of them. The third tank threw a track and was abandoned. Our M4 medium tanks fired 76mm on the German tank from about 400 yards. Three rounds ricocheted off. Later, on examination we found that the 76mm had penetrated only about two inches, just cutting a groove in the front slope.

Sloped armor on tanks provides little or no improvement over vertical armor when impacted by a shaped charged projectile. Only standoff armor, also known as spaced armor, could defeat shaped charged projectiles during World War II. Spaced armor is two armor plates, generally parallel, separated by an air space. The round detonates when it strikes the outer plate, and the shaped charge dissipates enough to prevent penetration.

The Germans mounted spaced armor on their Panzer III and IV medium tanks, primarily for protection from small-caliber AP projectiles. They experimented with spaced armor for the Tiger E tank but nothing ever came of it.

TIGER B TANK TURRETS

A description of one of the fifty Krupp-built turrets for the failed Porsche heavy tank chassis appears in a U.S. Army report dated September 13, 1944:

The turret, which is of exceptional length, is mounted centrally, and the side and rear plates are sloped at an angle of 25 degrees to the vertical. The side plates are bent inwards both at the front and at the rear and the top center of the near side turret wall bulges to the vertical to receive the cupola. There are no pistol ports or hatches in the side plates.

The front of the turret consists of a single plate which bends round the turret from the front end of

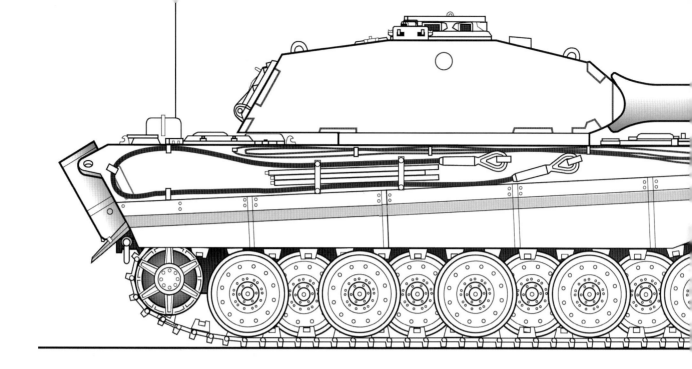

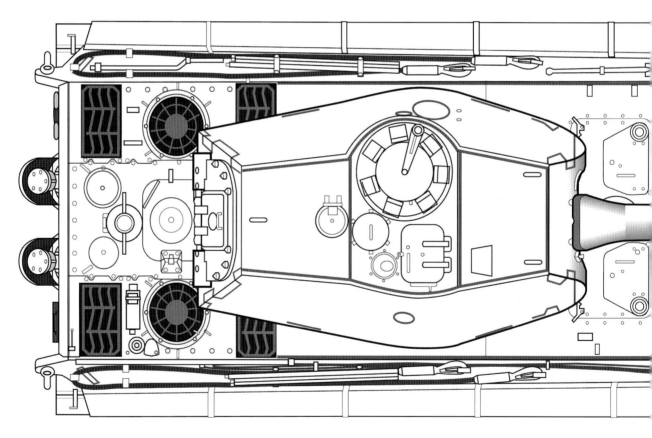

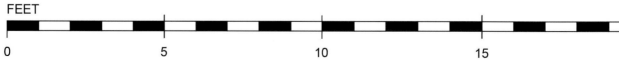

FEET

0   5   10   15

PzKpfw.Tiger Ausf. B

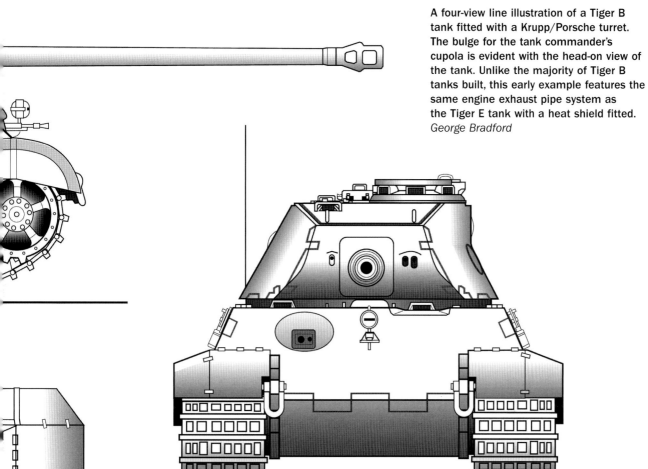

A four-view line illustration of a Tiger B tank fitted with a Krupp/Porsche turret. The bulge for the tank commander's cupola is evident with the head-on view of the tank. Unlike the majority of Tiger B tanks built, this early example features the same engine exhaust pipe system as the Tiger E tank with a heat shield fitted.
George Bradford

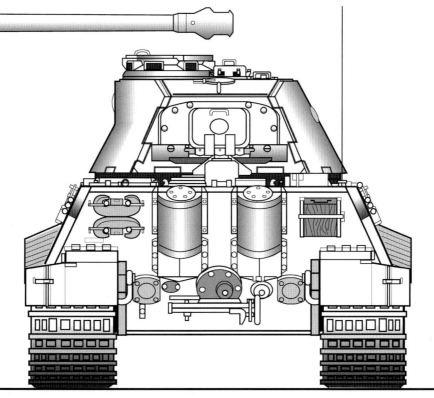

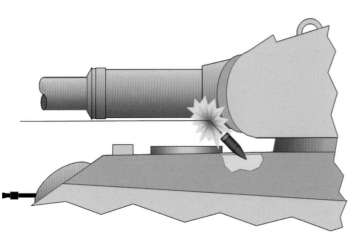

This illustration shows in more detail how the Krupp turret built for the failed *Porsche* chassis candidate for a new heavy tank, with the curved front armor plate and the curved armored gun shield, tended to deflect projectiles striking the front of the turret at a certain horizontal angle, downward into the thinner superstructure roof armor of the vehicle. *James D. Brown*

The Krupp turret built for the failed *Porsche* chassis candidate for a new heavy tank proved both complex and time consuming to build. Krupp therefore produced a redesigned turret (seen here) for the winning Henschel chassis candidate. The flat front turret plate (sloped at 10 degrees) simplified its production and did away with the shot trap on those turrets built for the *Porsche's* heavy tank chassis. *Frank Schulz*

the turret roof to a point on the turret base about three feet six inches from the front of the turret. This plate is 80mm [3.6 inches] thick from where it joins the forward edge of the turret front to a point immediately below this junction at the bottom of the turret front. It is then stepped down to 60mm [2.5 inches] and from here to its end it tapers down to 50mm [two inches]. The plate is dovetailed, interlocked, and welded to the turret side plates. At the point where the plate is stepped down from 80mm to 60mm, there is a large weld, incorporating a filling piece.

The arrangement of the armor at the bottom front of the Krupp/Porsche turret created a shot trap that deflected projectiles into the very thin superstructure roof just above the driver and radioman's positions. A U.S. Army report published after World War II defines the shot trap (reentrant angle):

A reentrant angle is an angle formed by surfaces of a vehicle such that an attack striking either surface may be ricocheted against the other surface. Such angles incorporated into the design of armored structures are undesirable from a protection standpoint.

Projectiles ricocheting from, or traveling along the surface of, reentrant angles may cause hits (by the projectile or fragments there from) on surfaces affording less protection, and which otherwise would be unexposed to attack. Sloping surfaces should be arranged so that impacting projectiles are not deflected into other areas of an armored vehicle.

The Krupp turret designed specially for the Henschel Tiger B tank chassis was superior to the Krupp turret for the failed Porsche tank design. It was cheaper, easier to build, and did away with the shot trap at the bottom of the front turret plate and the bulge on the left side of the turret for fitting the tank commander's cupola.

The almost-vertical turret RHA front plate on the Krupp/Henschel Tiger B tank turret was seven inches thick. The rounded CHA gun shield on the tank (designed to prevent shot traps) varied in thickness from three to four inches and covered most of the RHA front plate. It effectively pushed up the armor thickness on the front of the Krupp/Henschel Tiger B tank turret to almost twelve inches. The reason that the front of tank turrets needs to have the thickest armor possible appears in a passage from a pos-World War II U.S. Army report:

In order that fire may be brought to bear on the enemy, it is necessary that the turret be exposed, whereas a defilade position may be taken behind a hill, building, wall, or embankment which will provide partial or complete protection to the hull. Again, when operating in high grass or brush the turret will be the primary target visible to the enemy. It is therefore apparent that the gun shield and frontal areas of a turret will receive a high percentage of hits and therefore should offer as much or more protection than any other area on the front of a tank.

The RHA turret roof plate on the Krupp/Henschel Tiger B tank turret was an inch and a half thick. The frontal portion sloped at 78 degrees, the center portion was flat, and the rear portion sloped at 82 degrees. The three-inch side and rear plates were sloped at 25 degrees. The loader's overhead went from being a bit more than one-half-inch thick up to almost two inches thick beginning in July 1944.

The U.S. Army decided early in World War II that specialized tank destroyers would deal with German tanks. The M4 Sherman medium tank series, as seen here armed with a 75mm main gun, would be only a vehicle of exploitation. Events did not transpire that way, and Sherman tanks often found themselves forced into dealing with German Tiger tanks in unequal struggles. *Michael Green*

The U.S. Army's original solution for evening out the odds between M4 Sherman medium tanks and German tanks, like the Tiger, involved up-armoring them with a more powerful longer-barreled 76mm main gun, as seen here on this vehicle with a muzzle brake fitted. Sadly, combat experience quickly demonstrated that the new 76mm main gun still lacked the penetrative power needed to punch holes in Tiger tanks. *Michael Green*

ANOTHER PROTECTION FEATURE

A feature found on many Tiger E and Tiger B tanks was an antimagnetic mine paste, referred to in German as *Zimmerit,* that was normally applied at the factory. It went on the tanks because of the unfounded belief that Red Army infantrymen had magnetic antitank mines and would attach them to the sides of German tanks in battle. The purpose of the *Zimmerit* was to provide a magnetic gap between a tank's steel armor and the magnets attached to the bottom of the magnetic mines. It went on in two coats using metal racks that produced a rough finish, which magnetic mines would have problems adhering to. After application, the *Zimmerit* was hardened with blowtorches.

Zimmerit began to appear on new production Tiger E tanks in September 1943 and continued until production ceased in August 1944. In January 1944, an order when out to Tiger E tank units in the field to add *Zimmerit* to any tank that may have left the factory before September 1943. The Tiger B tank appeared with factory-applied *Zimmerit* beginning with the first series production vehicle in January 1944. Orders to discontinue applying *Zimmerit* at the factory appeared in September 1944 due to an unfounded belief that when struck by a large-caliber projectile, it had the potential to catch fire. Field units received instructions not to apply *Zimmerit* to any of their tanks starting in October 1944.

AMERICAN ENCOUNTERS WITH TIGER B TANK ARMOR PROTECTION

U.S. Army tank commander Sgt. Clyde D. Brunson, of the 2nd Armored Division, describes the effectiveness of the Tiger B tank armor in a wartime report:

> One day a Royal Tiger tank got within 150 yards of my tank and knocked me out. Five of our tanks opened up on him from ranges of 200 to 600 yards and got five or six hits on the front of the Tiger. They all just glanced off and the Tiger backed off and got away. If we had a tank like the Tiger, we would all be home today.

In the American army, it usually fell to the M4 series medium tanks to battle it out with the Tigers. Unfortunately, the fifteen-pound projectile of the M61 APC round fired from the 75mm gun on the M4 series tank traveled at only two thousand feet per second and just bounced off the Tiger B tank's frontal armor. The up-gunned M4 series tank, armed with a longer 76mm gun that fired a fifteen-pound projectile at 2,600 feet per second, could not even penetrate the frontal armor of

The only versions of the U.S. Army M4 Sherman medium tanks that mounted a main gun with sufficient penetrative powers to be able to defeat the thick armor on Tiger tanks proved to be those armed with the British army's tank gun version of their seventeen-pounder (76.2mm) antitank gun. An example of one of these tanks is on display at the Belgian Army Museum in Brussels. *David Marian*

the Tiger B tanks at point-blank range, as is recounted by Tech. Sgt. Dale Erickson in a wartime report: "Our tank guns, both 75mm and 76mm, haven't the penetrating power that the German tanks have. At Elbeuff, during August 1944, our AP shells bounced off a Mark VI at point blank range while we were on a road block."

First Lieutenant William L. Schabuel, U.S. Army, remarked in a wartime report that even with the most potent main gun round for the M4 Sherman tank—the *hyper*-velocity armor-piercing round (HVAP) with a tungsten-carbide-alloy subcaliber core—the Tiger B sloped turret and hull side plates were impenetrable:

At Oberment, Germany, 27 February 1945, our second platoon on road block was engaged by two

Tiger tanks, Mark VI. HVAP 76mm ammunition at 3,600 feet per second was used and bounced off the side slopes, seven rounds . . .

Upon throwing smoke at the Tiger tanks, they withdrew because smoke means marking target for artillery and fighter-bombers to the Germans.

The only M4 Sherman tank gun that could penetrate the armor of late-war German tanks was the seventeen-pound (76.2mm) gun. It was a British weapon, officially designated ordnance, quick firing (QF), seventeen-pounder, and when mounted in a Sherman tank, was listed in British wartime reports as the "Sherman seventeen-pounder" or some similar variation. In the decades after the war, it received the

Due to its impressive penetrative powers, the British army's seventeen-pounder (76.2mm) antitank gun went into a number of other tracked armored vehicles, including the U.S. Army's M10 tank destroyer, which the British army received in large numbers. Because the original main gun on the M10 tank destroyer lacked the penetrative power to kill Tiger tanks, the British army had it up-gunned with the seventeen-pounder, as seen here. *Michael Green*

name "Firefly." Offered to the U.S. Army, but refused, the American military later changed its mind and requested as many examples of Sherman tanks armed with a seventeen-pounder as possible. The war in Europe ended before any saw combat service, however.

The seventeen-pounder barrel was fifteen feet long. The gun fired two types of AP ammunition: A thirty-seven-pound, full-bore, armor-piercing, composite ballistic cap (APCBC) round with a seventeen-pound solid shot projectile that traveled to its target at 2,900 feet per second. In theory, it could penetrate about five inches of armor sloped at 30 degrees at a range of one thousand yards. The other, more potent, AP round for the seventeen-pounder was a twenty-eight-pound armor-piercing discarding sabot

(APDS) round. It contained a roughly eight-pound subcaliber, tungsten-alloy carbide core that traveled to its target at a muzzle velocity of 3,950 feet a second and could theoretically penetrate more than seven and a half inches of armor sloped at 30 degrees at a range of one thousand yards.

The discarding sabot on the seventeen-pounder APDS projectile separated from the projectile at the muzzle of the gun barrel. In contrast, the sabot of the APCR projectile fired from Tiger 8.8m guns traveled all the way to the target. The APDS subcaliber projectile thus offered a smaller frontal area for aerodynamic drag, and hence retained its kinetic energy over longer distances. In theory, the APCR subcaliber core fired from the seventeen-pounder could penetrate 7.6 inches of armor sloped at 30

No doubt, one of the most awkward-looking and ungainly tanks built for the British army during World War II was the Challenger. Despite its visual shortcomings, it did mount the seventeen-pounder and could kill a Tiger tank if given the chance. With the main gun pointed over the front hull, the vehicle was about 27 feet long; its width was 9 feet 6.5 inches and it was 9 feet tall. *Patton Museum*

degrees. Richard Hunnicutt, in his book *Sherman, A History of the American Medium Tank,* describes the disadvantages of the APCR projectile: "Unfortunately, the new shot was less accurate than the APCBC and some of the early production were particularly erratic, limiting their use to targets at fairly close range. However, they did provide a round capable of penetrating the heavy German armor then appearing on the battlefield."

The British also mounted the seventeen-pounder on a number of other armored fighting vehicles, including the four-man eighteen-ton turretless tank destroyer known as the Archer that used the chassis of the Valentine infantry support tank. The British army also removed the three-inch main guns from the thirty-three-ton diesel-powered American-supplied M10 turreted tank destroyers and replaced them with the seventeen-pounder. The rearmed M10 destroyers in British army service received the designation M10C or M10 seventeen-pounder.

The seventeen-pounder also appeared on a strange and ungainly looking tank known as the Challenger. The thirty-six-ton gasoline-powered vehicle had a crew of either four or five men and began entering service in late 1944. A somewhat more compact version of the seventeen-pounder gun—the Vickers high-velocity 75mm gun—had slightly less penetrative abilities than its larger counterpart. The Vickers gun appeared on a very successful gasoline-powered thirty-nine-ton tank with a five-man crew named the Comet, which entered British army service in December 1944.

U.S. ARMY TIGER TANK KILLERS

The only U.S. Army antitank gun that had a theoretical chance of penetrating the thick armor of the Tiger E and Tiger B tanks was the M3—a converted 90mm antiaircraft gun. It was the main weapon on both the M36 tank destroyer and M26 Pershing heavy tank (later designated a medium tank). In combat, it proved

The British army Comet tank seen here mounted a de-rated version of the seventeen-pounder antitank gun, normally referred to as a 77mm gun, which was still sufficient to hole a Tiger tank. The gun could penetrate more than five inches of armor at a range of 2,188 yards when firing an armor-piercing discarding sabot (APDS) round. *Michael Green*

to be somewhat of a disappointment. In a wartime report, Staff Sgt. Harvey W. Anderson compares his 90mm M3 gun's performance to that of the German Tiger tank's 8.8cm gun:

> I believe the 90mm gun on the T26 [M26] is almost comparable to the 88mm on the Mark VI but does not obtain the necessary muzzle velocity to penetrate the Mark V or the VI from the front. I have actually seen the 90mm Armor Piercing Cap [APC] bounce off a German VI at about 1,400 yards. In turn I have seen a German Mark VI with an 88mm KO [knock out] an American M4 at 3,300 yards with a ricochet hit through the side.

The American M3 90mm gun fired an M82 APC round that weighed almost forty-four pounds. The projectile portion of the M82 round weighed about

twenty-four pounds and had a muzzle velocity of 2,650 feet per second. A later version could reach 2,800 feet per second. It possessed more striking velocity than the 8.8cm APCBC projectiles fired from the Tiger E tank gun. (Striking velocity is the speed of a projectile when impacting a target.) Even with the higher striking velocity, the quality of the steel used in the projectile was inferior to the German rounds, so its penetration performance fell far short of the German projectiles.

For the M3 gun on the M26 Pershing Heavy Tank, the U.S. Army also provided HVAP (hyper-velocity armor piercing) rounds. The seventeen-pound tungsten subcaliber core projectile possessed a muzzle velocity of 3,350 feet per second.

Charles Geissel, a lieutenant in the U.S. Army 628th Tank Destroyer Battalion during World War II, recalls a combat encounter with a Tiger B tank late in 1944:

Our unit was one of a very few to be equipped with the M36 tank destroyer armed with a modified 90mm antiaircraft gun. Most other tank destroyer units had the M10 armed with a 3-inch modified naval gun. When we first received our M36s in England, we were told in classes that the 90mm gun mounted on our vehicle was far superior to the German 88mm gun. Yet, on my unit's first encounter with a Royal Tiger, our "B" company found their 90mm armor-piercing rounds wouldn't penetrate the turret armor of the German tank. It wasn't until a 90mm shell hit near the top of the vehicle's turret that a penetration was obtained. This round managed to set off a fire in the German tank and the crew then abandoned it. If I remember right, "B" company suffered several causalities during that brief

A restored M36 tank destroyer, with the paint scheme and markings from the U.S. Army in western Europe during World War II, is taking part in a military vehicle collector's rally in Belgium in 2006. It featured a powerful 90mm main gun intended to punch holes in Tiger tanks. However, combat experience showed this was not always the case. The first of these vehicles showed up in Europe in the fall of 1944. *David Marian*

Shown in this picture is one of the first of the U.S. Army's T26E3 (later M26) Pershing heavy tanks to arrive in Europe during World War II. The tank's 90mm main gun was the same as that mounted on the M36 tank destroyer. Because the Pershing tanks arrived in western Europe during the closing months of the war in Europe, in relatively small numbers, combat between them and Tiger tanks was limited to a couple of occasions. *Patton Museum*

shoot-out. Our unit encountered only one other Royal Tiger before the war ended. It also proved very difficult to destroy.

The M26 tank was the culmination of a long-range program that started in 1942 to develop a new tank to replace the M4 Sherman tank series. Until the first few weeks after the invasion of Europe on June 6, 1944, the M4 was considered an adequate weapon, so M26 development was given a very low priority. When the army finally realized that it needed a new tank with more firepower and better armor protection to match the Tiger E tank, the M26 had already been fitted with a 90mm gun and had grown to a weight of forty-six tons. Because of its weight, the M26 originally received a heavy tank designation. In contrast, the M4 Sherman medium tank weighed roughly thirty-three tons.

The U.S. Army had always acknowledged the superior firepower and protection levels of heavy tanks but

was reluctant to field one owing to their higher cost, diminished mobility, lower reliability, and transportation difficulties. The Germans had dealt with all these problems and more with Tiger tanks.

In February 1945, the U.S. Army rushed twenty M26 heavy tanks to western Europe. As foreseen, the M26 tank was difficult to get into battle because it could not cross the many delicate and narrow bridges in Europe, and it caused heavy damage to the army's existing portable bridges wherever they were deployed. It was also too wide for European railroads, so it needed dedicated tank transporters to move it from one battlefield to another.

The M26 tank saw only limited combat action against Tiger tanks owing to their late arrival in western Europe. One of the few encounters involving a Tiger E tank and an M26 Pershing (nicknamed "Fireball" by its crew) took place on February 25, 1945, near Elsdorf,

Germany. This excerpt from Richard Hunnicutt's book *Pershing: A History of the Medium Tank T20 Series* documents the battle:

The tank [M26] had been positioned behind a roadblock to watch for enemy movement. This turned out to be a poor location with the fires burning in the vicinity. In the darkness, flames from a burning coal pile silhouetted the turret, which was exposed above the roadblock. A German Tiger tank [Tiger E], concealed behind the corner of a building, fired three times at the turret at a range of about 100 yards. The first 8.8cm shot penetrated through the coaxial machine gun port and spun around inside the turret killing the gunner and the loader. The second hit the muzzle brake and the end of the gun tube jarring off the round that was in the chamber. The discharge of this shell caused the barrel to swell at about the halfway point even though the projectile went on out the tube. A third shot glanced off the upper right-hand side of the turret tearing away the cupola hatch cover, which had been left open. The Tiger then backed up, immobilizing itself on a pile of debris and was abandoned. The loader of the Tiger was later captured and confirmed that his tank had done the firing.

"Fireball" was promptly avenged the following day when Pershing number 40 assigned to Company E 33rd Armored Regiment knocked out and burned a Tiger I and two Panzer IVs, also at Elsdorf. Four shots were fired and registered on the Tiger at a range of approximately 900 yards. The first, a T30El6 HVAP projectile, destroyed the final drive. The second, a T33 shot, hit the bottom of the gun mantlet [gun shield] next to the hull penetrating the turret and causing an

Belonging to a private collector in Europe is this nicely restored M26 Pershing tank. To the U.S. Army tankers who went up against Tiger tanks in their under-gunned and under-armored M4 series Sherman medium tanks, the Pershing was a big improvement in armor protection and firepower and would have placed the American tankers on more even terms with the Tiger tanks. However, it showed up too late to make a difference. *Bob Fleming*

Pictured are two Tiger E tanks destroyed by their crews in order to prevent them falling into enemy hands. This proved to be the fate of far too many Tiger tanks plagued by mechanical shortcomings. The German failure to develop a suitable armored recovery vehicle able to deal with the weight of the Tiger tanks resulted in many of them being lost to breakdowns, which would have been repairable. *Patton Museum*

explosion. Two other hits by high explosive were ineffective. The two Panzer IVs were knocked out and burned at a range of 1,200 yards with one round each of T33, but an additional two rounds of high explosive were used to destroy the crews as they escaped.

Because the fifteen-and-a-half-foot M3 90mm gun mounted on the M26 tank could not effectively deal with the frontal armor on the Tiger B tank, the U.S. Army mounted a twenty-one-foot-long T15E1 90mm gun on an M26 tank and called it the "Super Pershing."

The T15E1 gun on the Super Pershing was equal in performance to the KwK 43, L/71 gun mounted in the Tiger B tank. The twenty-four-and-a-half-pound AP projectile, referred to as AP T43 Shot, achieved a muzzle velocity of 3,200 feet per second. The seventeen-pound HVAP projectile fired from the same gun achieved a muzzle velocity of 3,750 feet per second. This sole example of the Super Pershing was rushed to Germany in the very last days of the war in Europe with the hope of finding a Tiger B tank to fight. On April 22, 1945, in the Germany city of Dessau, the Super Pershing encountered a Tiger B tank as documented in an article

As the German military suffered constant setbacks on all fronts, the iron discipline of the early years disappeared and valuable pieces of military equipment, like the Tiger E tank pictured, fell into enemy hands undamaged to become objects of curiosity from the local inhabitants. *Patton Museum*

titled "Duel at Dessau" on The U.S. Army 3rd Armored Division History website:

> With 3rd AD [armored division] fanning out and the 36th Infantry riflemen following, the Super Pershing reached an intersection and began to round a corner to its right. Unknown to its crew, a King Tiger had apparently been waiting in ambush at a distance of a block or roughly 600 yards away, and in the same direction that the Americans were turning into.
>
> At this distance, easily within its capability, the Tiger fired at the Super Pershing. But its infamous high-velocity 88mm shell, of the type that had destroyed so many American tanks and vehicles during the war, went high and was not even close. Gunner Corporal John "Jack" Irwin, only 18 years old, responded almost instantly with a round that struck the Tiger's huge angled glacis (front plate.) But the shot, a non-armor-piercing high explosive

> (HE) shell, had no effect. Ricocheting off the armor, it shot skyward and exploded harmlessly. The Super Pershing had been loaded with an HE only because Irwin had been expecting urban targets, such as buildings, personnel, and light anti-tank guns. "AP!" he shouted to his loader Pete, which meant an armor-piercing shell would be next.
>
> Maduri [the tank commander] and crew then felt a concussion or thud on the turret. It was never known if this shot came from the Tiger, or from some other anti-tank weapon. In any case, no serious damage was done, probably a lucky glancing impact. In the next instant, Irwin aimed and fired a second time, just as the royal monster was moving forward and raising up over a pile of rubble. The 90mm AP round penetrated the Tiger's underbelly, apparently striking the ammo well and resulting in a tremendous explosion that blew its turret loose. With near certainty, the entire crew was killed. But, there was no

As the war in Europe entered its final few months and the German army began a desperate final defense of their country, German tanks, such as the abandoned Tiger E tank pictured, appeared only in very small numbers or singly. Allied air superiority and lack of fuel made any movement by German tanks an ordeal. *Patton Museum*

time to examine their "trophy." A battle was raging, and the Super Pershing continued down the street, passing the lifeless and burning King Tiger.

GERMAN AND SOVIET OPINIONS OF TIGER TANK ARMOR

Despite the impressive armor array on the Tiger tanks, it was obvious to some within the *Panzertruppen* ("tank troops") that their opponents were accelerating their development and fielding of ever more powerful tank and antitank guns. Tiger tank crews could no longer count on their armor protecting them on the battlefield, as is evidenced in this German army report released by the British army in June 1944:

When Tigers first appeared on the battlefield, they were in every respect proof against enemy weapons. They quickly won for themselves the title of "unbeatable" and "undamageable."

But in the meantime, the enemy had not been asleep. Antitank guns, tanks and mines have been developed, which can hit the Tiger hard, and even knock it out. Now the Tiger, for a long time regarded as a "life insurance policy," is relegated to the ranks of simply a heavy tank. No longer can the Tiger prance around oblivious of the laws of tank tactics. They must obey these laws, just as every other tank must.

So remember, you men who fight in Tiger tanks, don't demand the impossible from your Tiger.

Even the mighty Tiger B tanks eventually became prey to U.S. Army tanks or tank destroyer crews as is evident in this picture of a vehicle struck numerous times. The American soldier crouching on the superstructure roof of this tank points to one of two penetrations of the turret side armor. Another projectile has apparently cut the tracks on one side of the vehicle. *Patton Museum*

Do just what your commanding officer orders. He knows the limitations of his vehicle and guns, and he knows the best use to which they should be put.

The thoughts of the head of the German army tank troops on the protection levels of the Tiger tanks appeared in another British army report:

Faced as we are with the 122mm tank gun and 57mm antitank gun in Russia and the 92mm antiaircraft/antitank gun in Western Europe and Italy, "Tigers" can no longer afford to ignore the

principles practiced by normal tank formations. This means that "*Tigers*" can no longer show themselves on crests to have a look around but must behave like other tanks. Behavior of this kind caused the destruction by "Stalin" tanks of three "*Tigers*" recently, all crews being killed with the exception of two men.

This battalion was surely not unacquainted with the basic principle of tank tactic that tanks should only crest in a body and by rapid bounds, covered by fire, or else detour around the crest. The legend of the "thick hide," the "invulnerability" and the "safety"

The fate of those surviving Tiger tanks that did not fall prey to the scrap metal dealer's torches after World War II was to become the stars of attraction to generations of military buffs and modelers at military museums around the world. This Tiger B tank, with the Krupp-built turret for the failed Porsche chassis heavy tank, resides at the Tank Museum in Bovington, England. *Tank Museum, Bovington*

of the "Tiger," which has sprung up in other arms of the service, as well as within the tank arm, must now be destroyed and dissipated.

The Russian Battlefield (battlefield.ru) website contains this translation by Douglas Rauber of a Soviet army report on the armor testing of two captured Tiger B tanks in the fall of 1944.

The quality of armor on the "Tiger-B" tank compared with the armor on the "Tiger-I" and "Panther" tanks, as well as early production "Ferdinand" self-propelled guns, has sharply deteriorated. The first individual impacts caused cracks and spalling in the armor of the "Tiger-B" tank. Groups of shell impacts

(3–4 shells) caused large-scale spalling and fractures in the armor.

Weak weld seams appeared characteristic of all hull and turret joints. Despite careful workmanship, the seams held up to shell impacts significantly worse than they did in analogous constructions on the "Tiger-I" and "Panther" tanks as well as the "Ferdinand" self-propelled gun.

Impacts of three or four AP or HE fragmentation shells from 152, 122, or 100mm artillery pieces caused cracks, spalling and destruction of the weld seams in the tank's 100–190mm thick frontal armor plates at ranges of 500 to 1,000 meters. The impacts disrupted the operation of the transmission and took the tank out of service as an irrevocable loss.

INDEX

Other **Zenith Press** titles of interest to the enthusiast:

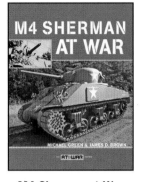
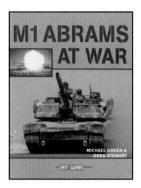
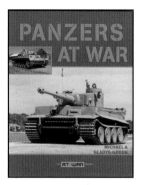
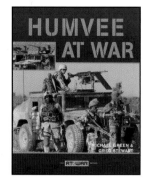
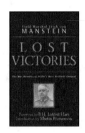
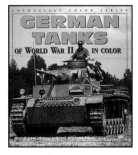
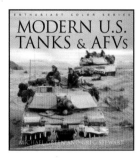

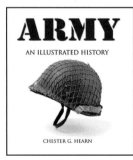

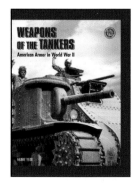